THE AUSTRALIAN
Women's Weekly

SUGAR FREE

CONTENTS

SUGAR ALTERNATIVES

Barley malt syrup

Barley malt syrup is made from sprouted (malted) barley, and produced in a similar way to rice malt syrup. This dark brown, unrefined sweetener, is thick and sticky with a distinct "malty" flavour, but is not as sweet as honey or table (white) sugar. Barley malt syrup is low in glucose, fructose and sucrose. It is available from health food stores.

Rice malt syrup

(BROWN RICE SYRUP)

Rice malt syrup is made by cooking brown rice flour with enzymes to break down the starch into sugars. The mixture is then filtered and the water removed to give a thick, sweet-tasting syrup. It is available from most major supermarkets and health food stores. Rice malt syrup is fructose-free and is a popular vegan alternative to honey.

Norbu

(MONK FRUIT SUGAR)

Monk fruit is a subtropical melon that has been grown for hundreds of years in South-East Asia. The fruit contains a group of sweet tasting antioxidant compounds. A little like stevia, these compounds deliver sweetness without the sugar and kilojoules. Monk fruit sugar has 96% fewer kilojoules than sugar, and will not affect blood glucose or insulin levels.

Honey

(RAW)

Honey is one of the most natural sweeteners we can use. And since honey bees make honey using the nectar from flowers, the local flora impacts on the flavour of the honey. Pure floral honeys have a low GI, but cheaper, blended honeys tend to be high. For a low GI honey look for Yellow Box, Stringy Bark, Red Gum, Iron Bark, Yapunya, Eucalypt or those labelled as pure floral honey.

Agave syrup

(AGAVE NECTAR)

Agave syrup is a sweetener produced from the agave plant (a succulent with thick fleshy leaves) in South Africa and Mexico. It has a low GI due to the high percentage of fructose present, which may be harmful if consumed in high quantities. Sweeter and slightly thinner than honey, agave syrup is another suitable vegan substitute for honey.

Stevia

Stevia comes from the leaves of a plant, so is promoted as a natural sweetener. It is hard to buy stevia in the traditional leaf form. Instead it is processed into a white powder that can be used in a similar way to sugar, a product which is highly refined. It has a minimal effect on blood glucose levels and has no kilojoules, so it can be a useful way to reduce your sugar intake.

Maple syrup

(PURE MAPLE SYRUP)

Pure maple syrup is the concentrated sap of the maple tree, whereas maple-flavoured syrups are usually just processed glucose syrup with added flavourings. Real maple syrup is much tastier and contains significant amounts of nutrients and antioxidant compounds. It has a low GI, making it a good choice for blood glucose control.

Coconut sugar

(COCONUT PALM SUGAR)

Coconut sugar is not made from coconuts, but from the sap of the blossoms of the coconut palm tree. The sap is collected and then boiled to evaporate the water content, leaving a sugar that looks a little like raw or light brown sugar with a similar caramel flavour. It also has the same amount of kilojoules as regular table (white) sugar.

Breakfast

mushroom & parmesan french toast

PREP + COOK TIME 15 MINUTES SERVES 2

2 eggs
½ cup (125ml) milk
2 teaspoons dijon mustard
¼ cup (20g) finely grated parmesan
4 x 2cm (¾-inch) thick slices sourdough bread
⅓ cup (80ml) olive oil
300g (9½ ounces) button mushrooms, sliced thinly
1 clove garlic, crushed
2 tablespoons fresh thyme leaves
2 teaspoons apple cider vinegar
10g (½ ounces) butter
¼ cup (60g) crème fraîche
¼ cup (20g) flaked parmesan
1 tablespoon finely chopped fresh chives

1 Using a fork, whisk eggs, milk, mustard and grated parmesan in a shallow dish until combined; season. Soak bread slices in egg mixture about 5 minutes, turning halfway through.

2 Meanwhile, heat 1½ tablespoons of the oil in a large frying pan over medium-high heat; cook half the mushrooms, without stirring, for 1 minute or until browned underneath. Cook, stirring, a further 2 minutes or until tender. Transfer to a heatproof dish; cover with foil. Repeat process with another 1½ tablespoons of the oil and remaining mushrooms, adding garlic and thyme during the last minute of cooking; stir in vinegar and half the butter. Combine all mushrooms in dish; cover to keep warm.

3 In same cleaned pan, heat remaining oil and remaining butter over medium heat; cook bread for 2 minutes each side or until golden.

4 Serve french toast topped with mushroom mixture, crème fraîche, flaked parmesan and chives.

Nutritional
COUNT PER SERVING

- ▶ 65.4g total fat
- ▶ 23.3g saturated fat
- ▶ 3482kJ (833 cal)
- ▶ 32.8g carbohydrate
- ▶ 27.7g protein
- ▶ 4.4g fibre

Test Kitchen
NOTES

We used a baby leaf micro herb mix of sorrel, parsley, coriander (cilantro) and radish. Leftover kale pesto can be stored, covered with a light layer of oil, in an airtight container in the fridge for up to 1 week.

breakfast salad with poached eggs & kale pesto

PREP + COOK TIME 25 MINUTES SERVES 2

¾ cup (45g) firmly packed baby leaves (see tips)
100g (3 ounces) brussels sprouts, shaved thinly
1 cup (150g) crunchy combo sprout mix
1 small carrot (80g), cut into matchsticks
2 tablespoons toasted sunflower seeds
2 tablespoons apple cider vinegar
1½ tablespoons avocado oil
1 teaspoon raw honey
1 tablespoon white vinegar
4 eggs
½ medium avocado (125g), sliced thinly

KALE PESTO
⅓ cup (55g) dry-roasted almonds
⅓ cup (50g) roasted cashews
2 small cloves garlic
2 cups (80g) baby kale, chopped coarsely
½ cup (125ml) extra virgin olive oil
1½ tablespoons apple cider vinegar
¼ cup (20g) finely grated parmesan

1 Make kale pesto.
2 Place baby leaves, brussels sprouts, sprout mix, carrot and seeds in a medium bowl; toss to combine. Whisk cider vinegar, 1 tablespoon of the oil and honey in a small bowl; season to taste. Add dressing to salad; toss to combine.
3 To poach eggs, half-fill a large, deep-frying pan with water, add white vinegar; bring to a gentle simmer. Break 1 of the eggs into a cup. Using a wooden spoon, make a whirlpool in the water; slide egg into whirlpool. Repeat with remaining eggs. Cook for 3 minutes or until whites are set and yolks are runny. Remove eggs with a slotted spoon; drain on a paper-towel-lined plate.
4 Divide salad between serving bowls; top with eggs and avocado. Spoon pesto on eggs; drizzle with remaining oil.

KALE PESTO Pulse nuts and garlic in a food processor until coarsely chopped. Add kale, oil and vinegar; pulse to a fine paste. Add parmesan, season with sea salt and cracked pepper; pulse until just combined. (Makes 1¼ cups)

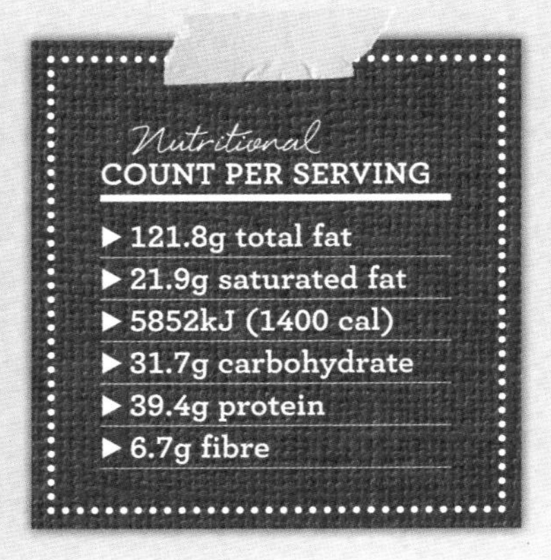

sweet potato rosti dukkah brunch

PREP + COOK TIME 30 MINUTES SERVES 2

240g (7½ ounces) purple-skinned white-flesh sweet potato, peeled, grated coarsely

1 medium onion (150g), grated coarsely

1 egg white

⅓ cup (25g) finely grated parmesan

1 tablespoon finely chopped fresh flat-leaf parsley

1 tablespoon finely chopped fresh dill

1 clove garlic, crushed

2 tablespoons olive oil

20g (¾ ounce) butter

1 tablespoon white vinegar

4 eggs

150g (4½ ounces) hot-smoked salmon, flaked

¼ cup (70g) Greek-style yoghurt

2 teaspoons dukkah

2 tablespoons fresh coriander (cilantro) leaves

lemon wedges, to serve

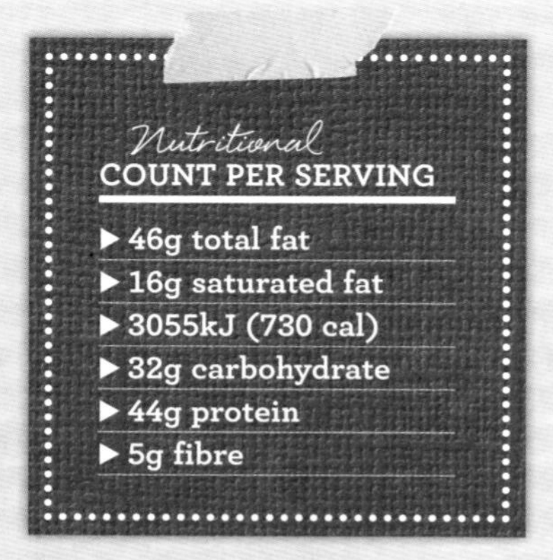

1 Preheat oven to 180°C/350°F. Line an oven tray with baking paper.

2 Combine sweet potato and onion in a medium bowl; squeeze out excess liquid, return vegetables to bowl. Stir in egg white, parmesan, herbs and garlic; season.

3 Heat half the oil and half the butter in a large frying pan over medium heat; spoon half the sweet potato mixture into pan, flatten to a 10cm (4-inch) round. Cook for 3 minutes each side or until golden. Drain on paper towel; place on tray, season with salt. Repeat with remaining oil, butter and sweet potato mixture to make two rosti in total.

4 Bake for 10 minutes or until crisp and cooked through.

5 Meanwhile, to poach eggs, half-fill a large, deep-frying pan with water, add vinegar; bring to a gentle simmer. Break 1 of the eggs into a cup. Using a wooden spoon, make a whirlpool in the water; slide egg into whirlpool. Repeat with remaining eggs. Cook for 3 minutes or until whites are set and yolks are runny. Remove eggs with a slotted spoon; drain on a paper-towel-lined plate.

6 Divide rosti between plates; top with salmon, eggs and yoghurt. Sprinkle with dukkah and coriander, serve with lemon wedges.

Test Kitchen NOTES

You can substitute kumara (orange sweet potato) or potato for the white sweet potato in the rosti and hot-smoked trout or white fish for the salmon. Dukkah is a Middle Eastern nut and spice mixture available from supermarkets and delis.

Test Kitchen NOTES

You can use grated apple or nashi instead of the pear. Look for freshly squeezed apple juices from single variety apples, such as granny smith, as they will have a clean fresh sweet and tart taste. Young drinking coconuts are available from green grocers and some supermarkets. To segment an orange, cut off the rind with the white pith, following the curve of the fruit. Cut down either side of each segment close to the membrane to release the segment.

quinoa & pear bircher with coconut fruit salad

PREP + COOK TIME 10 MINUTES SERVES 2

- 1 tablespoon pepitas (pumpkin seeds)
- 1 tablespoon sunflower seeds
- 1 medium pear (230g), grated coarsely
- 1½ cup (120g) quinoa flakes
- ½ cup (125ml) coconut milk
- ½ cup (125ml) unsweetened apple juice

COCONUT FRUIT SALAD

- 1 medium young drinking coconut (900g)
- 50g (1½ ounces) raspberries
- 60g (2 ounces) blueberries
- 1 tablespoon long thin strips of orange rind
- 1 medium orange (240g), peeled, segmented (see tips)

1 Make coconut fruit salad.

2 Stir pepitas and sunflower seeds in a small frying pan over medium heat for 2 minutes or until toasted.

3 Combine pear, quinoa, coconut milk, juice and reserved coconut water (from coconut fruit salad) in a medium bowl.

4 Divide bircher between two serving bowls; spoon fruit salad on top. Sprinkle with toasted seeds.

COCONUT FRUIT SALAD Insert the tip of a small knife into the soft spot on the base of the coconut, using a twisting action. Place coconut over a glass; drain coconut water. Reserve ½ cup (125ml) for bircher. Wrap coconut in a clean towel, break open with a hammer, or by smashing it onto the floor. Spoon out the soft coconut flesh; slice into thin strips. Combine coconut flesh with remaining ingredients in a small bowl. Cover; refrigerate until required.

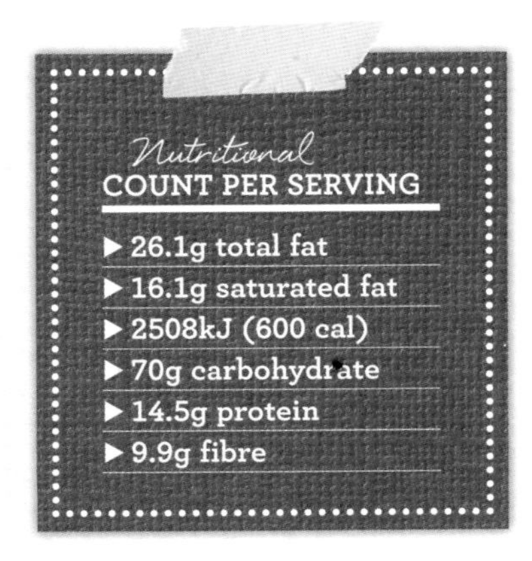

Store bircher in an airtight container in the refrigerator for up to 4 days.

banana pancakes with labne & blueberry compote

PREP + COOK TIME 40 MINUTES (+ STANDING) SERVES 4

You will need to start the labne 2 days ahead or serve the pancakes with Greek-style yoghurt.

1 medium ripe banana (200g)
¼ cup (35g) coconut flour
¼ teaspoon bicarbonate of soda (baking soda)
¼ teaspoon ground cinnamon
2 eggs
1 vanilla bean, split lengthways, seeds scraped
½ cup (125ml) unsweetened almond milk
2 tablespoons coconut oil
1 medium banana (200g), extra, sliced thickly
2 tablespoons roasted coconut chips

LABNE

500g (1 pound) Greek-style yoghurt
½ teaspoon sea salt
1 teaspoon finely grated lemon rind

BLUEBERRY COMPOTE

1 cup (250ml) apple juice
½ cup (75g) coconut sugar
2 cups (280g) frozen blueberries

1 Make labne.
2 Make blueberry compote.
3 Mash banana to a paste in a medium bowl with a fork. Add flour, soda, cinnamon, eggs, vanilla seeds and almond milk; stir to combine.
4 Melt one-third of the oil in a large non-stick frying pan over low-medium heat. Spoon tablespoons of batter into pan, flatten slightly; cook for 2 minutes or until bubbles appear on the surface. Using two spatulas, as mixture is delicate, carefully turn over; cook a further 1 minute or until cooked through. Remove from pan; keep warm. Repeat two more times with remaining coconut oil and batter to make 12 pancakes in total.
5 Serve pancakes topped with labne, extra banana, coconut chips and blueberry compote.

LABNE Line a sieve with two layers of muslin (or a clean Chux cloth); place it over a bowl. Stir ingredients together in a small bowl; spoon into the lined sieve. Tie muslin close to the surface of yoghurt; refrigerate 48 hours. (Makes 260g/8½ ounces)

BLUEBERRY COMPOTE Stir juice and sugar in a medium saucepan over low heat until sugar dissolves. Bring to a simmer; cook for 10 minutes or until reduced to a thin syrup. Add blueberries; stir gently until berries are coated and thawed.

Nutritional
COUNT PER SERVING

- 24.3g total fat
- 15.8g saturated fat
- 2337kJ (559 cal)
- 69.2g carbohydrate
- 14.3g protein
- 3.5g fibre

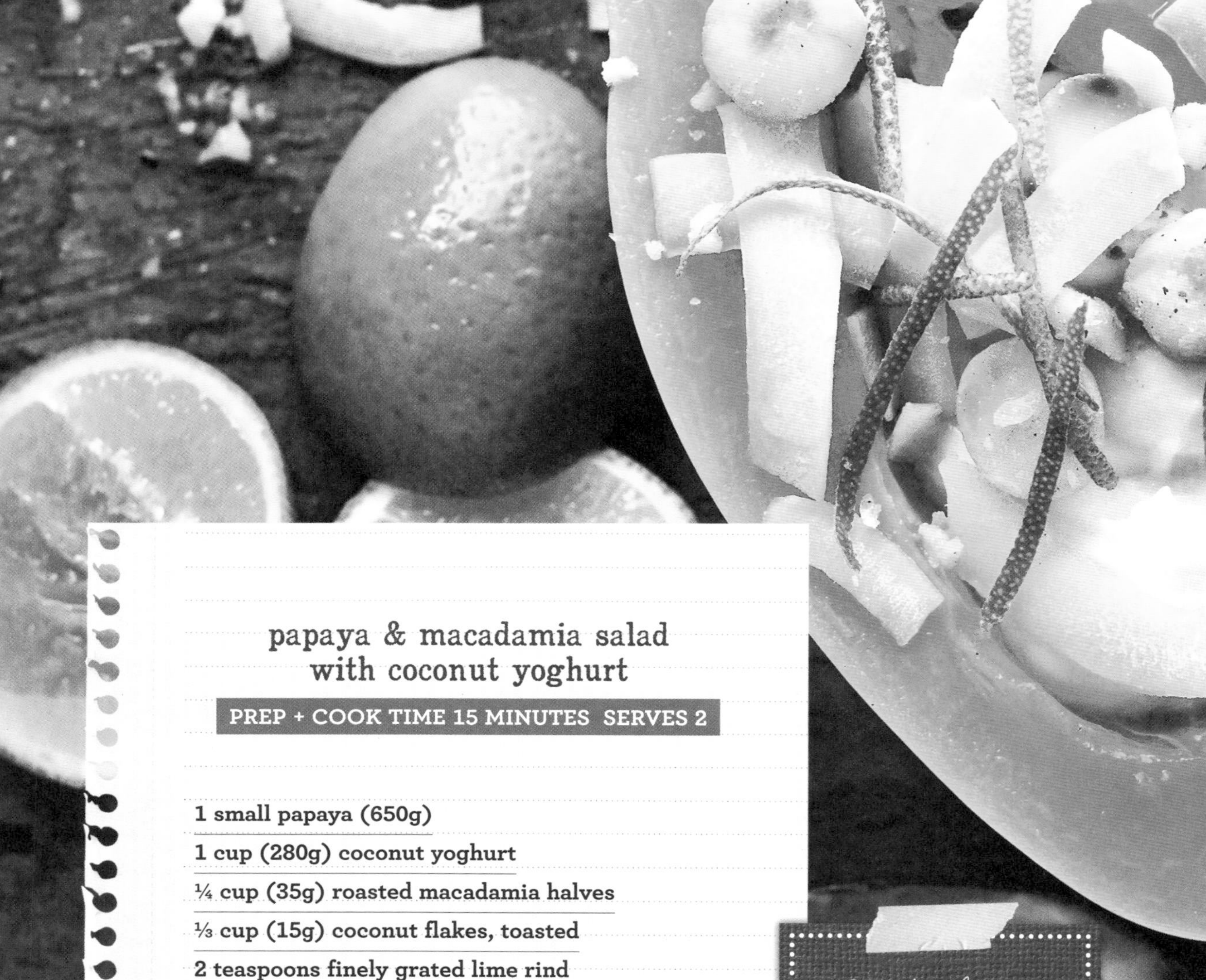

papaya & macadamia salad with coconut yoghurt

PREP + COOK TIME 15 MINUTES SERVES 2

- 1 small papaya (650g)
- 1 cup (280g) coconut yoghurt
- ¼ cup (35g) roasted macadamia halves
- ⅓ cup (15g) coconut flakes, toasted
- 2 teaspoons finely grated lime rind
- 2 limes (180g), cut into wedges

1 Cut papaya in half lengthways; scoop out seeds.
2 Spoon yoghurt into papaya hollow; sprinkle with macadamias, coconut and rind.
3 Serve immediately with lime wedges.

Nutritional
COUNT PER SERVING

- 41g total fat
- 24g saturated fat
- 2052kJ (490 cal)
- 23.5g carbohydrate
- 4.9g protein
- 6.3g fibre

super seed bowl with apple & yoghurt

PREP + COOK TIME 10 MINUTES SERVES 2

- 2 medium green apples (300g), cut into matchsticks
- 2 tablespoons lemon juice
- ½ cup (125ml) coconut water
- 100g (3 ounces) strawberries, sliced thickly
- ½ cup (140g) Greek-style yoghurt
- 2 tablespoons raw honey

SUPER SEED MIX

- 2 tablespoons each sunflower seeds and pepitas (pumpkin seeds)
- 1½ tablespoons each sesame seeds, poppy seeds, chia seeds and linseeds (flaxseeds)
- 2 tablespoons currants
- 2 tablespoons goji berries

1 Make super seed mix.

2 Combine apple and juice in a medium bowl.

3 Divide apple mixture and half the seed mix between two bowls, add coconut water. Top with strawberries and yoghurt; drizzle with honey and sprinkle with remaining seed mix.

SUPER SEED MIX Stir sunflower seeds and pepitas in a small frying pan over medium heat for 2 minutes or until lightly golden. Add sesame seeds, poppy seeds, chia seeds and linseeds; stir for 30 seconds or until all are toasted. Remove from pan; cool. Stir in currants and goji berries. (Makes 1 cup)

Nutritional COUNT PER SERVING

- 31.2g total fat
- 6.2g saturated fat
- 2596kJ (621 cal)
- 65.9g carbohydrate
- 18.1g protein
- 9.4g fibre

Test Kitchen
NOTES

When in season, use pears instead of apples. Super seed mix can be made ahead. Store in an airtight container or jar in the fridge for up to 3 months.

Test Kitchen
NOTES

Try to buy a kumara with a diameter of 7cm (2¾ inches), as it will provide the base for your stack, and tomatoes of a similar size. If green heirloom tomatoes are hard to find, use red. Target beetroots are available from specialist green grocers and grower's markets. If they're unavailable, use radishes or shaved fennel.

vegie & egg power stack

PREP + COOK TIME 40 MINUTES SERVES 4

400g (12½ ounces) medium kumara (orange sweet potato) (see tips)

8 fresh shiitake mushrooms (140g), stems trimmed

¼ cup (60ml) olive oil

2 teaspoons chopped fresh rosemary

1 long fresh red chilli, seeded, chopped

2 tablespoons sunflower seeds

2 cups (80g) baby kale

¼ cup (20g) finely grated parmesan

1 tablespoon white vinegar

8 fresh eggs

3 green heirloom tomatoes (380g), sliced (see tips)

4 baby target beetroot (beets) (80g), sliced thinly (see tips)

½ cup baby micro cress

LEMON AÏOLI

1 egg yolk

1 small clove garlic, chopped

1 tablespoon finely grated lemon rind

1 teaspoon fresh chopped rosemary

2 tablespoons lemon juice

½ teaspoon raw honey

½ cup (125ml) olive oil

Nutritional
COUNT PER SERVING

- 56g total fat
- 11g saturated fat
- 2969kJ (709 cal)
- 27g carbohydrate
- 22.5g protein
- 6.6g fibre

1 Preheat oven to 200°C/400°F. Line an oven tray with baking paper.

2 Cut kumara into eight 5mm (¼-inch) thick rounds. Place on tray with mushrooms, 2 tablespoons of the oil, rosemary and chilli; toss to coat. Bake for 25 minutes or until kumara is tender.

3 Meanwhile, make lemon aïoli.

4 Heat remaining oil in a medium frying pan over medium heat; cook sunflower seeds, stirring, for 2 minutes or until toasted. Stir in kale, turn off heat; leave for the residual heat to wilt leaves. Add parmesan; season to taste.

5 To poach eggs, half-fill a large, deep-frying pan with water, add vinegar; bring to a gentle simmer. Break 1 of the eggs into a cup. Using a wooden spoon, make a whirlpool in the water; slide egg into whirlpool. Repeat with 3 more eggs. Cook eggs for 3 minutes or until whites are set and yolks are runny. Remove eggs with a slotted spoon; drain on a paper-towel-lined plate. Keep warm. Repeat poaching with remaining eggs.

6 Spoon 2 tablespoons of the aïoli onto each plate. Build two stacks on each plate with kumara, tomato, mushrooms then kale mixture. Top each stack with a poached egg, sliced beetroot and micro cress.

LEMON AÏOLI Process egg yolk, garlic, rind, rosemary, juice and honey in a small food processor about 1 minute. With motor operating, gradually add oil, drop by drop at first, then in a slow steady stream until mixture is thick and emulsified. Season to taste. (Makes ⅔ cup)

The unused vanilla pod can be wrapped and frozen for up to 1 year. Use in recipes where a vanilla bean is called for.

strawberry & almond sweet frittata

PREP + COOK TIME 30 MINUTES SERVES 4

250g (8 ounces) strawberries, hulled

1 tablespoon coconut sugar

1 vanilla bean, split lengthways, seeds scraped

6 eggs

2 tablespoons coconut sugar, extra

⅓ cup (40g) ground almonds

10g (½ ounce) butter

100g (3 ounces) firm ricotta, crumbled coarsely

⅓ cup (55g) dry-roasted almonds, chopped coarsely

1 Thinly slice half the strawberries; cut remaining strawberries in half. Combine halved strawberries with sugar in a small bowl. Reserve sliced strawberries.

2 Place vanilla seeds, eggs, extra sugar and ground almonds in a medium bowl; whisk until combined.

3 Preheat grill (broiler) to high.

4 Melt butter in a 24cm (9½-inch) non-stick ovenproof frying pan over medium heat. Add egg mixture, top with sliced strawberries, ricotta and half the chopped almonds. Reduce heat to low; cook, for 8 minutes or until half set. Place pan under grill a further 8 minutes or until ricotta is lightly browned and mixture just set.

5 Serve immediately topped with halved strawberries and remaining chopped almonds. Drizzle with some honey and sprinkle with black chia seeds, if you like.

Store muesli in an airtight container in the fridge for up to 4 weeks.

grain-free coconut & vanilla muesli

PREP + COOK TIME 30 MINUTES (+ COOLING)
SERVES 4 (MAKES 4¾ CUPS)

- 2 vanilla beans
- 2½ cups (125g) flaked coconut
- ½ cup (80g) natural almonds, chopped coarsely
- ½ cup (80g) brazil nuts, chopped coarsely
- ½ cup (60g) pecans, chopped coarsely
- ¼ cup (35g) sunflower seeds
- ½ cup (100g) virgin coconut oil, melted
- 2 tablespoons raw honey
- ½ teaspoon sea salt

1 Preheat oven to 160°C/300°F. Grease and line two large oven trays with baking paper.
2 Split vanilla beans in half lengthways; using the tip of a small knife, scrape out seeds. Place seeds and pods in a large bowl with remaining ingredients; stir to combine. Spread mixture evenly between trays.
3 Bake for 20 minutes, stirring occasionally to break into clumps, or until lightly golden. Cool.

Nutritional
COUNT PER SERVING

- ▶ 88.8g total fat
- ▶ 49g saturated fat
- ▶ 3916kJ (935 cal)
- ▶ 21.5g carbohydrate
- ▶ 12.6g protein
- ▶ 5.6g fibre

banana & choc-almond toastie

PREP + COOK TIME 15 MINUTES MAKES 2

- **4 square slices packaged sourdough bread (180g) (see tips)**
- **10g (½ ounce) butter, softened**
- **2 tablespoons almond butter**
- **1 teaspoon cacao powder**
- **2 teaspoons rice malt syrup**
- **1 medium banana (180g), sliced thinly**
- **¼ teaspoon ground cinnamon**

1 Preheat a jaffle or sandwich maker.

2 Spread one side of each bread slice with butter.

3 Stir almond butter, cacao and syrup in a small bowl until smooth.

4 Place two slices of bread buttered-side-down on a board; spread half the almond butter mixture on each slice, then top with banana, leaving a 1cm (½-inch) border. Top with remaining bread slices, buttered-side-up.

5 Cook sandwiches in jaffle maker for 5 minutes or until golden. Serve cut in half, dusted with cinnamon.

Test Kitchen NOTES

You can use any bread you prefer – wholemeal, wholegrain and rye would all taste great, however they need to be square to fit a jaffle maker. You can substitute any nut butter of your choice for the almond butter. Other great alternatives are coconut butter or ricotta.

green quinoa with sesame eggs

PREP + COOK TIME 25 MINUTES SERVES 2

½ cup (100g) white quinoa, rinsed
1 cup (250g) chicken or vegetable stock
4 eggs, at room temperature
2 teaspoons coconut oil
1 small clove garlic, crushed
1 fresh small red chilli, chopped finely
2 cups (80g) thinly sliced kale (see tip)
2 cups (90g) firmly packed thinly sliced silver beet (see tip)
1 tablespoon lemon juice
¼ cup finely chopped fresh flat-leaf parsley
1 tablespoon white sesame seeds
1 tablespoon black sesame seeds
1 teaspoon sea salt flakes

1 Place quinoa and stock in a medium saucepan; bring to the boil. Reduce heat to low-medium; simmer gently for 15 minutes or until most of the stock is absorbed. Remove from heat; cover, stand 5 minutes.
2 Meanwhile, cook eggs in a small saucepan of boiling water about 5 minutes. Remove from pan; cool under cold running water 30 seconds. Peel.
3 Heat oil in a medium saucepan over medium heat, add garlic and chilli; cook stirring, for 2 minutes or until fragrant. Add kale and silver beet; stir until wilted. Stir in quinoa and juice; season to taste.
4 Combine parsley, sesame seeds and salt in a small bowl. Roll peeled eggs in parsley mixture.
5 Serve quinoa topped with eggs.

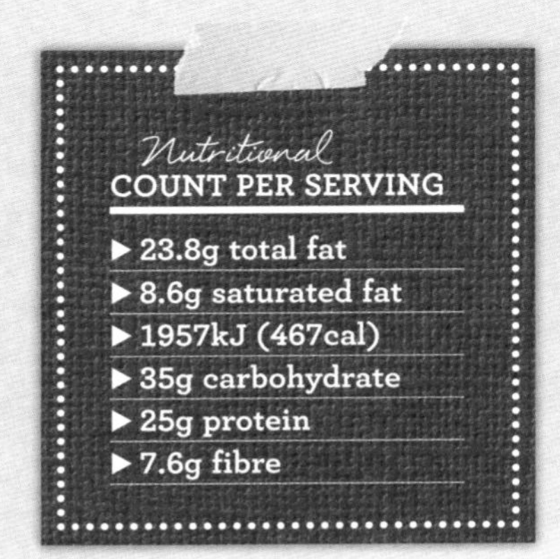

DRINKS

berry berry luscious

PREP TIME 10 MINUTES MAKES 3 CUPS

Soak 2 tablespoons goji berries in 1 cup chilled coconut milk blend (see tip) in a small bowl about 10 minutes. Transfer to a high-speed blender; add 2 cups frozen mixed berries, 1 cup firmly packed baby spinach and 1 extra cup chilled coconut milk blend. Blend until smooth. Serve over ice, topped with 1 tablespoon each goji berries and mixed berries.

TIP We used Pureharvest Coco Quench, a blend of coconut and rice milks; it has a thinner consistency than canned coconut milk but still tastes the same.

electrolyte booster

PREP TIME 10 MINUTES MAKES 1 LITRE

Blend 2 cups coconut water, 400g (12½ ounces) frozen pineapple, 1 small avocado (200g), ½ trimmed, chopped baby fennel (65g), ½ cup fresh mint leaves, 2 cups firmly packed baby spinach and 2 tablespoons lime juice in a high-speed blender until smooth. Serve over ice.

TIP Frozen pineapple is available from supermarkets or you can freeze your own portioned, peeled, cored and chopped pineapple in zip-top bags.

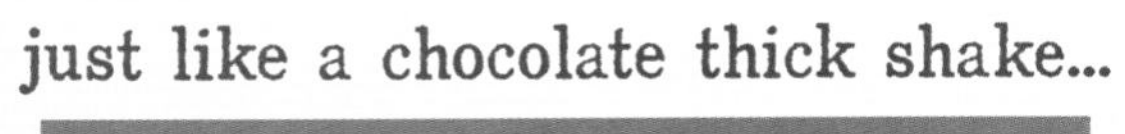

just like a chocolate thick shake...

PREP TIME 10 MINUTES MAKES 1 LITRE

Blend 2 cups unsweetened almond milk, 2 ripe medium (260g) chopped frozen bananas, 1 small (200g) chopped avocado, 1 cup firmly packed baby spinach, 2 tablespoons cacao powder, ⅓ cup vanilla bean whey protein powder or yoghurt and 1 tablespoon raw honey in a high-speed blender until smooth. Serve over ice, dusted with ¼ teaspoon extra cacoa powder.

green tea & kiwi sipper

PREP TIME 10 MINUTES (+ COOLING)

MAKES 1 LITRE

Brew 2 green tea bags in 2 cups boiling water about 5 minutes. Discard tea bags. Stir in 1 tablespoon raw honey. Cool in refrigerator. Place cooled tea in a high-speed blender with 1 cup frozen green grapes, 2 medium (170g) peeled chopped kiwi fruit, 1 cup fresh mint leaves and 1 cup firmly packed baby spinach until smooth. Serve immediately over ice.

TIP This drink separates quickly, so it is best made just before serving.

Mains

chilli lime snapper with corn salsa salad

PREP + COOK TIME 35 MINUTES SERVES 4

¼ cup (60ml) olive oil
1 clove garlic, sliced thinly
1 fresh long green chilli, seeded, chopped finely
1 teaspoon finely grated lime rind
4 x 180g (5½-ounce) boneless, skinless snapper fillets
2 corn cobs (250g), husks removed
6 red radishes (90g), sliced thinly
45g (1½ ounces) snowpea sprouts, trimmed
1 green onion (scallion), sliced thinly
¼ cup fresh coriander (cilantro) leaves
1 tablespoon lime juice
1 tablespoon white balsamic vinegar or white vinegar
1 tablespoon olive oil, extra
1 medium avocado (250g), sliced
lime wedges, to serve

1 Combine 2 tablespoons of the oil with garlic, chilli and rind in a small bowl; add snapper, turn to coat. Set aside.

2 Brush corn with remaining oil; cook on a heated chargrill plate (or barbecue), turning every 2 minutes, for 8 minutes or until corn is cooked and lightly charred. Cool.

3 Place radish, sprouts, onion and coriander in a bowl of iced water to crisp.

4 Cut kernels from cooled cobs; place in a large bowl with juice, vinegar and extra oil. Remove radish mixture from water with a slotted spoon; drain on paper towel. Add to corn mixture, season to taste; toss gently to combine.

5 Line same chargrill plate with baking paper (ensure paper doesn't extend over the edge); cook snapper on heated plate, for 2 minutes each side or until just cooked through.

6 Serve snapper with corn salsa salad, avocado and lime wedges.

Nutritional
COUNT PER SERVING
▶ 32.3g total fat
▶ 6g saturated fat
▶ 2465kJ (589 cal)
▶ 25.5g carbohydrate
▶ 44.5g protein
▶ 8.9g fibre

Nutritional
COUNT PER SERVING
▶ 30.5g total fat
▶ 10g saturated fat
▶ 2128kJ (509 cal)
▶ 32g carbohydrate
▶ 21.2g protein
▶ 3.5g fibre

quinoa, kale & fetta patties

PREP + COOK TIME 1 HOUR (+ STANDING & REFRIGERATION) SERVES 6

Prepared relishes and chutney contain sugar so there's a good reason to make your own. Our quick version uses the natural sweetness of beetroot.

¾ cup (150g) quinoa, rinsed

1¼ cups (310ml) water

1 small zucchini (90g), grated coarsely

1 teaspoon fine sea salt

120g (4 ounces) fetta, crumbled coarsely

¾ cup (80g) parmesan, grated finely

3 eggs, beaten lightly

1 cup (35g) loosely packed shredded curly kale

⅓ cup coarsely chopped fresh flat-leaf parsley

½ cup (35g) day-old sourdough breadcrumbs

1 clove garlic, crushed

2 teaspoons finely grated lemon rind

¼ cup (60ml) olive oil

4 wholegrain barley wraps (180g)

½ cup (140g) Greek-style yoghurt

1 medium lemon (140g), cut into wedges

BEETROOT RELISH

1 teaspoon cumin seeds

1 medium beetroot (beet) (175g), cut into thin matchsticks

¼ cup (60ml) sherry vinegar

½ medium red onion (75g), sliced thinly

2 tablespoons extra virgin olive oil

1 tablespoon fresh thyme leaves

1 Place quinoa and the water in a small saucepan over medium heat; bring to the boil. Reduce heat to low; cook, covered, for 15 minutes or until water is absorbed. Remove from heat; stand covered, 10 minutes. Spread over a tray; cool.

2 Combine zucchini and salt in a small sieve over a small bowl; stand 30 minutes.

3 Meanwhile, make beetroot relish.

4 Squeeze zucchini to remove excess liquid. Combine zucchini, quinoa, fetta, parmesan, egg, kale, parsley, breadcrumbs, garlic and rind in a medium bowl; season. Cover; refrigerate 1 hour.

5 Preheat oven to 160°C/325°F. Line an oven tray with baking paper.

6 Shape firmly packed ⅓-cup of mixture with wet hands into patties; place on tray. Cover; refrigerate 1 hour to firm.

7 Heat half the oil in a large frying pan over medium heat; cook half the patties, for 3 minutes each side or until golden and cooked through. (Take care turning the patties as the mixture is quite delicate.) Transfer to the oven tray; keep warm in the oven. Repeat with remaining oil and patties.

8 Serve quinoa patties with beetroot relish, wraps, yoghurt and lemon wedges.

BEETROOT RELISH Stir cumin seeds in a small frying pan over medium heat for 30 seconds or until fragrant and toasted. Pound seeds in a mortar and pestle until coarsely crushed. Transfer to a medium bowl; stir in remaining ingredients until combined. Season to taste.

glazed chicken on noodles

PREP + COOK TIME 1 HOUR SERVES 4

4 chicken breast supremes (720g) (see tips)

2 tablespoons rice bran oil

1 medium mandarin (200g), unpeeled, cut into four thick slices

4 cloves garlic, sliced thinly

2 long fresh red chillies, seeded, cut into matchsticks

300g (9½ ounces) leeks, trimmed, cut into matchsticks

270g (8½ ounces) dried udon noodles

2 green onions (scallions), sliced on the diagonal

¼ cup fresh coriander (cilantro) sprigs

GLAZE

⅓ cup (80ml) soy sauce

⅓ cup (80ml) chinese cooking wine (shao hsing)

2½ tablespoons raw honey

2 teaspoons finely grated mandarin rind

⅓ cup (80ml) mandarin juice

2 teaspoons finely grated ginger

½ teaspoon ground cinnamon

¼ teaspoon ground star anise

1 Preheat oven to 200°C/400°F. Line an oven tray with baking paper.

2 Make glaze.

3 Rub chicken with half the oil; season. Heat a large non-stick frying pan over medium heat; cook chicken for 5 minutes each side or until skin is golden. Transfer chicken to tray; brush glaze on both sides. Dip mandarin slices in glaze; place on chicken. Bake for 15 minutes, brushing with glaze halfway though cooking, or until chicken is cooked through. Cover; keep warm.

4 Heat remaining oil in same frying pan over medium heat; cook garlic and chilli about 1 minute. Add leek; cook a further 5 minutes or until soft.

5 Meanwhile, cook noodles in a saucepan of boiling water for 10 minutes or until tender; drain, reserving ¼ cup of the cooking water.

6 Add noodles and reserved cooking water to pan with onion and coriander; season, then toss to coat. Divide noodle mixture among shallow serving bowls; top with chicken and mandarin, drizzle with remaining glaze.

GLAZE Bring ingredients to a simmer in a small saucepan; cook for 5 minutes or until mixture thickens.

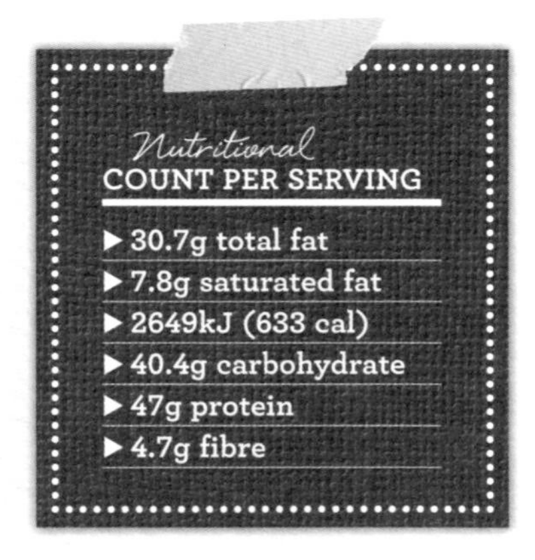

Test Kitchen

NOTES

Chicken breast supreme is a chicken breast with the skin and wing bone attached. Ask the butcher to prepare it for you or use skinless chicken breast fillets instead. You can use any Asian-style noodles you prefer. Toss noodles with 1 teaspoon rice bran oil after cooking if you are not using them immediately.

Test Kitchen NOTES

To bruise garlic, place the flat side of a cook's knife on the unpeeled clove; using the heel of your other hand push down on the knife to flatten it. Remove the skin. Reserve poaching liquid for another use; store in the refrigerator for up to 3 days.

fennel, apple & pistachio chicken salad

PREP + COOK TIME 25 MINUTES (+ COOLING) SERVES 4

When poaching chicken, it is easy to overcook it and make it tough. The secret to keeping it tender and moist is to finish off the cooking in the gentle residual heat of the pan. This method also works well when you are cooking fish.

2 cups (500ml) chicken stock
2 cups (500ml) water
4 thin slices lemon
4 cloves garlic, bruised (see tip)
6 fresh thyme sprigs
2 x 200g (6½-ounce) chicken breasts
½ cup (125ml) lemon juice
1 tablespoon dijon mustard
⅓ cup (80ml) extra virgin olive oil
1 small fennel (130g), sliced thinly
1 medium apple (150g), sliced thinly
1 cup (40g) trimmed watercress
1 cup firmly packed fresh flat-leaf parsley leaves
1 cup firmly packed torn fresh mint
1 medium avocado (250g), sliced thinly
½ cup (60g) pistachios, crushed coarsely

1 Place stock, the water, lemon slices, garlic and thyme in a medium saucepan over medium heat. Add chicken; bring to the boil. Reduce heat; simmer about 4 minutes. Cover pan, turn off heat; set aside to cool to room temperature. Remove chicken; shred coarsely.
2 Whisk juice and mustard in a small bowl until combined; gradually whisk in oil until combined. Season to taste.
3 Combine fennel, apple, watercress, herbs and avocado in a large bowl. Add chicken and dressing; toss to combine. Season to taste. Serve salad topped with pistachios.

Nutritional
COUNT PER SERVING

- 41.7g total fat
- 7.7g saturated fat
- 2268kJ (542 cal)
- 11g carbohydrate
- 28g protein
- 7.2g fibre

seeded cauliflower falafel

PREP + COOK TIME 1 HOUR SERVES 6 (MAKES 30 FALAFEL)

- ½ cup (100g) pepitas (pumpkin seeds)
- ½ cup (75g) sunflower seeds
- ¼ cup (35g) sesame seeds
- 2 tablespoons linseeds (flaxseeds)
- 700g (1½ pounds) cauliflower, cut into florets
- 2 cloves garlic, crushed
- 1½ tablespoons cumin seeds, crushed
- 1½ tablespoons coriander seeds, crushed
- ½ cup loosely packed fresh mint leaves
- ½ cup loosely packed fresh flat-leaf parsley leaves
- ½ cup (140g) tahini
- 2 tablespoons psyllium husks (see tips)
- 2 tablespoons lemon juice
- ¼ cup (60ml) water
- rice bran oil, for deep-frying

SALAD

- 1 small red onion (100g), sliced thinly into rings
- 250g (8 ounces) grape tomatoes, sliced crossways
- ¼ cup (60ml) red wine vinegar
- 140g (4½ ounces) persian fetta

HUMMUS

- 400g (12½ ounces) canned chickpeas (garbanzo beans), undrained
- ¼ cup (70g) tahini
- 1 clove garlic
- 1½ tablespoons lemon juice
- 1 teaspoon cumin seeds, crushed

1 Make salad and hummus.

2 Heat a medium frying pan over medium-high heat, add pepitas, sunflower seeds, sesame seeds and linseeds; cook, stirring, for 2 minutes or until sesame seeds are golden.

3 Process toasted seeds with cauliflower and remaining ingredients (except rice bran oil) to a coarse paste; season well. Line an oven tray with baking paper. Using a dessert spoon, scoop up a mound of mixture. Hold a second dessert spoon the same size upside down and drag it over the falafel mixture in an arc shape as you reach the other side, bring the top of the spoon under the scoop of falafel mixture transferring it onto it in the process. Using the first spoon, push the quenelle-shaped falafel onto the tray.

4 Fill a medium saucepan two-thirds full with oil, heat to 160°C/325°F (or until oil sizzles when a small cube of bread is added). Fry, six falafel at a time, for 5 minutes or until dark golden and cooked through. Drain on paper towel.

5 Spoon hummus onto plates, top with falafel and salad. Sprinkle with extra mint and parsley leaves, if you like.

SALAD Place onion, tomato and vinegar in a small bowl; stand 30 minutes. Stir in fetta.

HUMMUS Process chickpeas and canning liquid with remaining ingredients for 3 minutes or until smooth.

Test Kitchen
NOTES

Pysllium husks are obtained from the seeds of a plant native to India. They are useful for their binding qualities and are a good source of dietary fibre. Buy at vitamin and health food shops.

Nutritional
COUNT PER SERVING

- 50.7g total fat
- 9.5g saturated fat
- 2629kJ (629 cal)
- 15.8g carbohydrate
- 23.1g protein
- 12.6g fibre

Nutritional
COUNT PER SERVING
▶ 28.5g total fat
▶ 6g saturated fat
▶ 1606kJ (384 cal)
▶ 17.7g carbohydrate
▶ 10g protein
▶ 8g fibre

zucchini & ricotta fritters with carrot relish

PREP + COOK TIME 40 MINUTES SERVES 4

- 600g (1¼ pounds) zucchini, grated coarsely
- 1 tablespoon sea salt flakes
- 2 cloves garlic, crushed
- 2 green onions (scallions), chopped finely
- 2 tablespoons coarsely chopped fresh mint
- 2 eggs
- 2 teaspoons finely grated lemon rind
- ¾ cup (90g) ground almonds
- ½ cup (120g) firm ricotta
- ¼ cup (60ml) olive oil
- 100g (3 ounces) baby rocket (arugula)

CARROT RELISH

- 2 tablespoons olive oil
- 2 cloves garlic, crushed
- ¼ teaspoon chilli flakes
- 3 medium carrots (360g), cut into thin matchsticks
- ¼ cup (40g) currants
- 2 tablespoons norbu (monk fruit sugar)
- ¼ cup (60ml) red wine vinegar
- ½ cup (125ml) water
- 1 teaspoon ground cardamom
- 400g (12½ ounces) vine-ripened tomatoes, seeded, chopped coarsely

1 Combine zucchini and salt in a medium bowl. Stand 15 minutes.

2 Meanwhile, make carrot relish.

3 Squeeze excess liquid from zucchini. Combine zucchini with garlic, onion, mint, eggs, rind, ground almonds and ricotta in a medium bowl; season.

4 Heat half the oil in a large frying pan over medium heat. Pour heaped ¼-cup of fritter mixture into pan; cook for 3 minutes each side or until golden and cooked through. Remove from pan; cover to keep warm. Repeat with remaining oil and fritter mixture, to make 12 fritters in total.

5 Serve fritters topped with relish and rocket.

CARROT RELISH Heat oil in a large frying pan over medium-high heat; cook garlic and chilli flakes about 30 seconds. Add carrot; cook about 3 minutes. Stir in currants, norbu, vinegar, the water and cardamom; cook for 6 minutes or until liquid has evaporated. Stir in tomato; cook a further 2 minutes or until softened slightly. Season. Cool.

The relish can be stored for up to 2 weeks in an airtight container in the fridge.

persian sabzi pumpkin salad

PREP + COOK TIME 1 HOUR SERVES 4

- 1.2kg (2½ pounds) jap pumpkin
- ⅓ cup (80ml) extra virgin olive oil
- 2 teaspoons finely grated lemon rind
- 2 tablespoons lemon juice
- 4 radishes (60g), sliced thinly
- 2 green onions (scallions), sliced thinly
- ¼ cup loosely packed fresh basil leaves
- ¼ cup loosely packed fresh coriander (cilantro) leaves
- ¼ cup loosely packed fresh mint leaves
- ¼ cup fresh dill sprigs
- 4 lebanese flatbread pockets (320g)
- 1 cup (280g) store-bought labne
- 250g (8 ounces) baby roma (egg) tomatoes, sliced crossways (see tips)
- ⅓ cup (45g) coarsely chopped pistachios

ADVIEH SPICE MIX

- 2 teaspoons dried rose petals
- 1 teaspoon caraway seeds
- 1 teaspoon ground cinnamon
- 1 teaspoon ground nutmeg
- 1 teaspoon ground cardamon
- ½ teaspoon ground cumin
- ½ teaspoon ground cloves

1 Preheat oven to 220°C/425°F. Line two oven trays with baking paper.

2 Make advieh spice mix.

3 Wash, halve and remove seeds from pumpkin; cut into 12 wedges. Divide wedges between oven trays. Drizzle with 2 tablespoons of the oil, season on both sides with 2 teaspoons advieh spice mix and salt and pepper. Bake for 40 minutes or until pumpkin is golden and skin is crisp at the edges.

4 Whisk remaining oil with rind and juice in a small bowl; season to taste.

5 Soak radish and onion in iced water 5 minutes; drain, dry on paper towel. Place radish and onion in a medium bowl with herbs; toss gently to combine.

6 Toast flatbreads in the oven about 3 minutes. Place breads on plates; spread with labne. Top with pumpkin, tomato and herb salad; sprinkle with pistachios, drizzle with dressing.

ADVIEH SPICE MIX Grind rose petals and caraway seeds with a mortar and pestle until a coarse powder. Stir in remaining spices.

Test Kitchen
NOTES

You can make your own labne using the recipe on page 14. We used a mix of tomato varieties for extra colour; halve, quarter and slice the tomatoes depending on their size. Advieh is an aromatic Persian spice mix that can be used to season vegetables, meat or fish.

Gazpacho can be made up to 2 days ahead, store in an airtight container in the fridge; stir before serving.

green gazpacho with pistachio croutons

PREP + COOK TIME 30 MINUTES (+ REFRIGERATION) SERVES 6

- 1 medium avocado (250g), chopped
- 50g (1½ ounces) baby spinach
- 360g (11½ ounces) honeydew melon, chopped coarsely
- ¼ cup loosely packed fresh basil leaves
- 2 cloves garlic, crushed
- 10 green onions (scallions), white part only, chopped coarsely
- 200g (6½ ounces) seedless green grapes
- 2 fresh long green chillies, chopped coarsely
- 750g (1½ pounds) green heirloom tomatoes, chopped coarsely
- 1 telegraph cucumber (400g), chopped coarsely
- 2 tablespoons white wine vinegar
- ¼ cup (60ml) extra virgin olive oil
- 8 ice cubes
- ¼ cup small fresh basil leaves, extra

PISTACHIO CROUTONS

- ¼ cup (60ml) olive oil
- 1 clove garlic, crushed
- 4 slices seeded rye bread (260g), cut into 1cm (½-inch) cubes
- ¼ cup (35g) pistachios, chopped

1 Make pistachio croutons.

2 Blend avocado, spinach, melon, basil, garlic, onion, grapes, chilli, tomato and cucumber, in two batches. Strain through a fine sieve over a large bowl, pressing down to extract as much liquid as possible. Discard solids. Whisk in vinegar, half the oil and ice cubes; season to taste. Refrigerate 30 minutes or until chilled.

3 Serve gazpacho in chilled bowls or glasses, topped with croutons, extra basil and remaining oil.

PISTACHIO CROUTONS Heat oil in a small frying pan over medium heat; cook garlic about 30 seconds. Add bread and pistachios; cook, stirring, for 5 minutes or until golden. Cool.

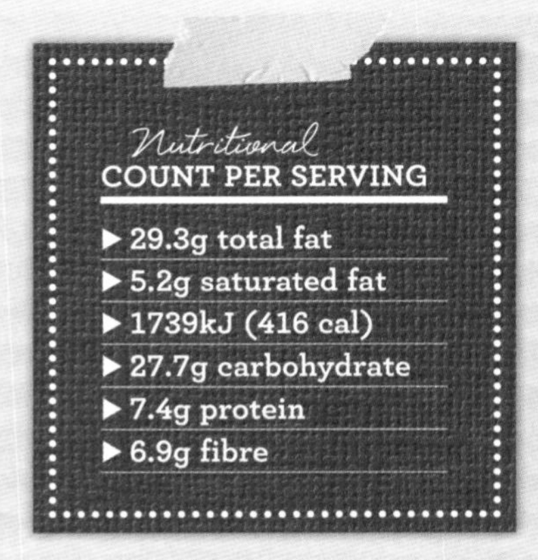
Nutritional COUNT PER SERVING

- 29.3g total fat
- 5.2g saturated fat
- 1739kJ (416 cal)
- 27.7g carbohydrate
- 7.4g protein
- 6.9g fibre

prawn chu chee curry with roti bread

PREP + COOK TIME 1 HOUR SERVES 6

- 2 cups (400g) medium-grain brown rice
- 1 litre (4 cups) water
- ½ teaspoon salt
- ¼ cup (60g) ghee
- 2½ tablespoons thai red curry paste
- 1kg (2 pounds) uncooked prawns (shrimp), peeled, deveined, with tails intact
- 6 fresh kaffir lime leaves
- 270ml coconut milk
- 1 cup (250ml) fish stock
- 2 tablespoons coconut sugar
- 2 tablespoons fish sauce
- 1 tablespoon tamarind puree
- 225g (7 ounces) canned bamboo shoots, drained, rinsed
- ½ cup (85g) chopped fresh pineapple
- 1 fresh long red chilli, seeded, shredded finely

ROTI BREAD

- 1 teaspoon raw honey
- ¾ cup (180ml) warm water
- ¼ cup (60ml) milk
- ⅓ cup (80ml) rice bran oil
- 1 egg
- 3 cups (450g) white spelt flour
- 1 teaspoon salt
- 60g (2 ounces) ghee

1 Make roti bread.

2 Rinse rice in a sieve under cold water until water runs clear. Place rice in a medium saucepan with the water and salt; bring to the boil. Reduce heat to low; cook, covered, for 25 minutes or until water is absorbed. Remove from heat; stand, covered, 5 minutes. Fluff with a fork and keep warm.

3 Meanwhile, heat a wok over medium-high heat. Add ghee and paste; cook, stirring, about 2 minutes. Add prawns and 3 crushed lime leaves; cook, stirring, about 2 minutes. Add coconut milk and stock; simmer about 5 minutes. Add sugar, sauce and tamarind. Stir in bamboo shoots and pineapple; cook a further 2 minutes or until warmed though.

4 Finely shred remaining lime leaves; combine with chilli. Sprinkle lime leaf mixture on curry; serve with rice and warm roti bread.

ROTI BREAD Dissolve honey in a jug with the warm water, milk and 2 tablespoons of the oil; whisk in egg. Process flour and salt until combined. With the motor operating, gradually add milk mixture; process until a sticky dough forms. Knead dough on a floured surface for 2 minutes or until smooth. Divide into six portions; roll into balls. Place balls in a medium bowl with remaining oil, turn to coat well. Pat a ball of dough out on a lightly oiled surface until 20cm (8-inch) round. Using oiled hands, carefully stretch dough out from the centre in a circular motion, until dough is translucent and forms a 40cm (16-inch) round (don't worry if the dough rips, this will add texture). Fold each side into the centre to form a 15cm (6-inch) square; do not press. Place on a baking-paper-lined oven tray. Repeat with remaining dough. Heat 2 teaspoons of the ghee in a large frying pan over medium heat; cook roti, in batches, for 2 minutes each side or until golden, adding remaining ghee with each batch.

Nutritional
COUNT PER SERVING

- ▶ 44.4g total fat
- ▶ 22.7g saturated fat
- ▶ 4201kJ (1005 cal)
- ▶ 115.9g carbohydrate
- ▶ 34.3g protein
- ▶ 3.5g fibre

Test Kitchen
NOTES

Dashino-moto stock powder is Japanese stock powder, made from bonito (tuna) and konbu (seaweed). It is used to make dashi, a stock that forms the base of many recipes. Eggs can steep in the reduction for up to 48 hours for a deep rich flavour. Unpeeled eggs can be stored in an airtight container in the fridge for up to 4 days.

Nutritional
COUNT PER SERVING

- 9.6g total fat
- 2.4g saturated fat
- 1124kJ (269 cal)
- 23.6g carbohydrate
- 16g protein
- 6.2g fibre

eastern mash-up ramen

PREP + COOK TIME 2 HOURS (+ REFRIGERATION) SERVES 4

You will need to start this recipe a day ahead.

1 litre (4 cups) chicken stock

10g (½ ounce) dashino-moto stock powder (see tips)

3 cups (750ml) water

3 cloves garlic, sliced thinly

¼ cup (60ml) soy sauce

2 tablespoons sake

1 teaspoon norbu (monk fruit sugar) or stevia granules

20g (¾-ounce) piece fresh ginger, sliced

1 long fresh red chilli, quartered lengthways

300g (9½ ounces) buckwheat soba noodles

2 green onions (scallions), cut into thin strips

3 sheets toasted nori (seaweed), quartered

1 teaspoon black sesame seeds

TEA EGGS

3 cups (750ml) water

1 cup (250ml) soy sauce

¼ cup (20g) black tea leaves

4 star anise

rind of 1 mandarin

4 eggs, from the fridge

KIMCHI

250g (8 ounces) baby cucumbers (qukes)

¼ cup (50g) norbu (monk fruit sugar)

2 tablespoons salt

¼ cup (60ml) boiling water

2 green onions (scallions), chopped coarsely

1 teaspoon finely grated ginger

1 clove garlic

1 fresh long green chilli, sliced thinly

2 tablespoons rice vinegar

1 teaspoon fish sauce

1 tablespoon soy sauce

1½ tablespoons sesame seeds, toasted

1 Make tea eggs.

2 Place stock, dashino-moto, the water, garlic, sauce, sake, norbu, ginger and chilli in a saucepan; bring to the boil. Reduce heat; simmer about 30 minutes.

3 Meanwhile, make kimchi.

4 Cook noodles in a saucepan of boiling water for 6 minutes or until just tender; drain.

5 Peel and halve tea eggs. Divide noodles and broth among bowls; top with eggs, kimchi, onion and nori, sprinkle with sesame seeds.

TEA EGGS Bring the water, sauce, tea, star anise and rind to the boil in a medium saucepan. Reduce heat; simmer about 1 hour. Cool. Cook eggs in a small saucepan of boiling water about 7 minutes. Run eggs under cold water to stop them continuing to cook. Crack shell all over, but do not peel. Place eggs in cooled tea mixture. Cover; refrigerate overnight.

KIMCHI Cut cucumbers in half lengthways; cut crossways into 5mm (¼-inch) slices. Stir norbu, salt and the boiling water until dissolved. Place cucumber and salt mixture in a plastic zip-top bag, expel air; seal. Lie bag flat 30 minutes. Meanwhile, process remaining ingredients until finely chopped; spoon into a small bowl. Drain cucumbers; rinse, pat dry with paper towel. Add to bowl; toss to combine.

olive chicken with maple-roasted vegetables

PREP + COOK TIME 1 HOUR 50 MINUTES SERVES 4

- ¼ cup (60ml) olive oil
- 1 whole chicken (1.6kg), cut into 10 pieces
- 1 medium brown onion (150g), chopped coarsely
- 2 cloves garlic, crushed
- 3 sprigs fresh thyme
- 18 sicilian green olives (90g)
- 1 litre (4 cups) chicken stock
- 1 tablespoon lemon juice

MAPLE-ROASTED VEGETABLES

- 600g (1¼ pounds) kent pumpkin, cut into 2cm (¾-inch) wedges
- 4 small parsnips (480g), unpeeled, quartered lengthways
- 400g (12½ ounces) spring onions, trimmed to 10cm (4-inch) lengths, quartered lengthways
- 2 tablespoons extra virgin olive oil
- 2 tablespoons pure maple syrup
- 1 cup (40g) loosely packed rocket (arugula) leaves
- 1 tablespoon lemon juice

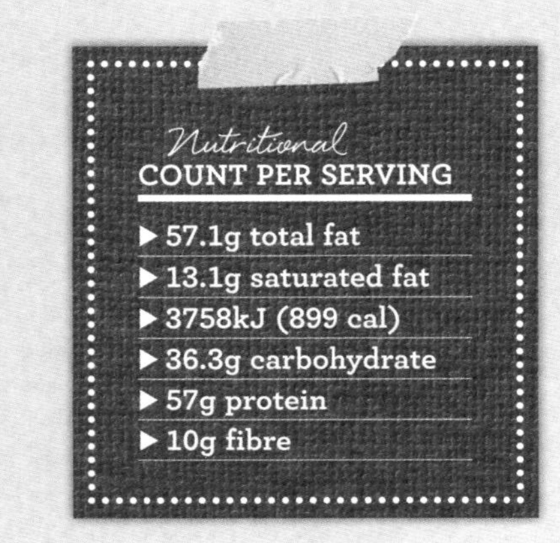
Nutritional COUNT PER SERVING

- 57.1g total fat
- 13.1g saturated fat
- 3758kJ (899 cal)
- 36.3g carbohydrate
- 57g protein
- 10g fibre

1 Heat oil in a large heavy-based saucepan over high heat; cook chicken, in batches, for 2 minutes each side or until browned. Remove from pan.

2 Reduce heat to medium; cook onion, garlic, thyme and olives in same pan, stirring occasionally, for 5 minutes or until onion is softened. Increase heat to high; return chicken and any juices to pan. Add stock; bring to the boil. Reduce heat to low; simmer, covered, for 1 hour or until chicken is cooked through. Remove chicken from pan.

3 Meanwhile, preheat oven to 200°C/400°F; make maple-roasted vegetables.

4 Increase saucepan heat to high; bring to the boil. Reduce heat slightly; cook, uncovered, for 20 minutes or until liquid has reduced to 1 cup (250ml). Add juice, season to taste.

5 Serve chicken with reduced mixture and maple-roasted vegetables.

MAPLE-ROASTED VEGETABLES Line two oven trays with baking paper. Divide pumpkin, parsnip and onion between trays; drizzle with oil and maple syrup, season, then toss to coat. Roast for 40 minutes, turning halfway through cooking, or until vegetables are tender. Combine rocket and lemon juice in a medium bowl; season to taste. Just before serving, toss rocket through vegetables.

Test Kitchen
NOTES

Sicilian olives contain pits, so warn your guests before eating or use pitted olives instead.

Nutritional
COUNT PER SERVING
▶ 34.2g total fat
▶ 10g saturated fat
▶ 2725kJ (652 cal)
▶ 59.1g carbohydrate
▶ 23.3g protein
▶ 6g fibre

sweet potato gnocchi with roasted tomato sauce

PREP + COOK TIME 2 HOURS SERVES 4

580g (1¼ pounds) purple-skinned white-fleshed sweet potato

170g (5½ ounces) fresh firm ricotta

½ cup (40g) finely grated parmesan

1 teaspoon ground nutmeg

1 teaspoon sea salt

1 egg

1 cup (150g) spelt flour

2 tablespoons olive oil

¼ cup (20g) flaked parmesan

¼ cup loosely packed small fresh basil leaves

ROASTED TOMATO SAUCE

500g (1 pound) vine-ripened tomatoes, halved

6 cloves garlic, unpeeled

1 large red capsicum (bell pepper) (350g), chopped coarsely

1 medium red onion (170g), cut into wedges

1 tablespoon fresh oregano leaves

1 tablespoon fresh lemon thyme leaves

1 tablespoon fresh rosemary leaves

¼ cup (60ml) extra virgin olive oil

2 tablespoons sugar-free balsamic vinegar

1 teaspoon pure maple syrup

¼ cup loosely packed fresh basil leaves

¼ cup (20g) finely grated parmesan

1 Preheat oven to 200°C/400°F.

2 Wrap sweet potato in foil; bake for 1½ hours or until tender.

3 Meanwhile, make roasted tomato sauce.

4 Combine ricotta, grated parmesan, nutmeg, salt and egg in a large bowl until smooth. Cut sweet potato in half lengthways; spoon flesh into a small bowl, mash with a fork. Add hot sweet potato to ricotta mixture; combine well. Stir flour into sweet potato mixture to form a firm dough.

5 Bring a large saucepan of salted water to the boil. Divide dough into eight portions. Using floured hands, roll each portion on a floured surface into a 2cm (¾-inch) thick sausage shape; cut into 4cm (1½-inch) lengths. Squeeze gnocchi in the middle to form a bow shape. Place gnocchi, in a single layer, on an oven tray dusted with flour.

6 Cook gnocchi in boiling water, in three batches, for 2 minutes or until they float to the surface. Remove with a slotted spoon to an oiled tray. Reserve ½ cup of the cooking water; stir into roasted tomato sauce.

7 Heat oil in a large frying pan over high heat; cook gnocchi, tossing occasionally, for 5 minutes or until lightly golden. Stir roasted tomato sauce into gnocchi to combine. Serve gnocchi topped with flaked parmesan and basil.

ROASTED TOMATO SAUCE Line a large roasting pan with baking paper. Add tomato, garlic, capsicum, onion, herbs and 2 tablespoons of the oil; season, toss to coat. Roast for 1 hour or until vegetables are very tender. Squeeze garlic from skins onto vegetables. Transfer mixture to a medium saucepan, add vinegar, maple syrup, remaining oil, basil and parmesan; season. Using a stick blender, blend sauce until smooth. Keep warm over a low heat.

quinoa crusted kale & fig tart

PREP + COOK TIME 1 HOUR 30 MINUTES (+ REFRIGERATION) SERVES 6

¾ cup (150g) tri-coloured quinoa, rinsed
1½ cups (120g) finely grated pecorino cheese
3 eggs
1 teaspoon sea salt flakes
1 tablespoon olive oil
1 clove garlic, crushed
3 cups (70g) firmly packed coarsely chopped kale
¼ cup (60ml) water
1 tablespoon dijon mustard
¾ cup (180ml) pouring cream
10 medium figs (600g), torn in half
1 cup (40g) loosely packed rocket (arugula) leaves
¼ cup (35g) roasted hazelnuts, halved

YOGHURT DRESSING
⅓ cup (95g) Greek-style yoghurt
1 teaspoon raw honey
2 teaspoons chopped fresh tarragon
½ clove garlic, crushed

1 Grease an 11cm x 35cm (4½-inch x 14-inch) rectangular loose-based tart tin.
2 Cook quinoa in a large saucepan of boiling water for 12 minutes or until tender; drain well. Cool.
3 Process quinoa and half the pecorino until quinoa is finely chopped. Add 1 of the eggs and half the salt; process until mixture forms a coarse dough. Press mixture evenly over base and sides of tart tin. Refrigerate 30 minutes or until firm.
4 Meanwhile, preheat oven to 200°C/400°F.
5 Bake tart shell for 30 minutes or until golden. Remove from oven; reduce temperature to 180°C/350°F.
6 Meanwhile, heat oil in a medium frying pan over medium heat; cook garlic about 30 seconds. Add kale; cook, stirring, about 30 seconds. Add the water; cook, covered, about 3 minutes. Remove from heat; stand, covered, 1 minute. Cool; drain away any excess liquid.
7 Place kale mixture in a medium bowl with remaining eggs and salt, mustard, cream and half the remaining pecorino; whisk to combine. Spread mixture evenly into tart shell; sprinkle with remaining pecorino.
8 Bake for 30 minutes or until filling is set. Place figs, cut-side up, on an oiled oven tray; bake alongside tart, for 30 minutes or until just soft.
9 Make yoghurt dressing.
10 Serve tart topped with figs, rocket and hazelnuts; drizzle with yoghurt dressing.

YOGHURT DRESSING Combine ingredients in a small bowl; season to taste.

Nutritional
COUNT PER SERVING
- 28g total fat
- 12.6g saturated fat
- 1852kJ (442 cal)
- 30g carbohydrate
- 16.5g protein
- 4.5g fibre

Test Kitchen
NOTES

We used crème fraîche in the crab filling rather than a commercial aïoli or mayonnaise as they tend to contain refined sugars.

prawn & crab sweet potato sliders

PREP + COOK TIME 35 MINUTES MAKES 12

The sweet potatoes need to be about 7cm (2¾ inches) in diameter as they will serve as the 'buns' for the sliders.

3 purple-skinned white-fleshed sweet potatoes (1kg), unpeeled

¼ cup (60ml) olive oil

12 large green king prawns (shrimp) (300g), peeled, deveined, with tails intact

2 cups (50g) watercress sprigs

¼ cup fresh micro sorrel leaves

¼ cup fresh coriander (cilantro) leaves

1 tablespoon extra virgin olive oil

1 tablespoon lemon juice

1 medium avocado (250g)

CRAB FILLING

200g (6½ ounces) cooked crab meat

½ cup (60g) crème fraîche

½ clove garlic, crushed

1 green onion (scallions), chopped finely

1 tablespoon finely chopped fresh chives

1 tablespoon nigella seeds

2 tablespoons horseradish cream

1 tablespoon lemon juice

1 Cut eight 8mm (½-inch) thick rounds, from each sweet potato (you need 24 rounds in total); discard tapered ends. Brush rounds with 2 tablespoons of the olive oil; season. Cook rounds, in batches, on a heated chargrill plate (or barbecue) for 6 minutes each side or until cooked through. Remove from heat; keep warm.

2 Make crab filling.

3 Coat prawns in remaining olive oil; season. Cook prawns on heated chargrill plate for 1 minute each side or until just cooked through. remove from heat; cover to keep warm.

4 Place watercress, sorrel and coriander in a small bowl with extra virgin olive oil and juice. Season; toss to combine. Mash avocado in a small bowl.

5 Place 12 sweet potato rounds on a board; top each with crab filling, a prawn, mashed avocado and watercress salad. Top with remaining sweet potato rounds.

CRAB FILLING Combine ingredients in a small bowl; season.

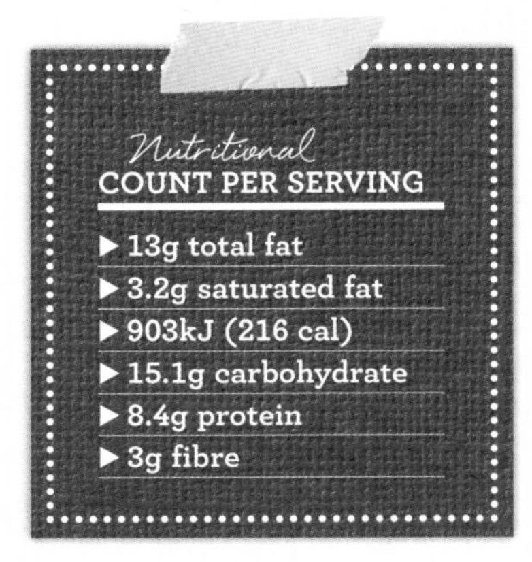

healthy kedgeree

PREP + COOK TIME 50 MINUTES SERVES 4

1.5 litres (6 cups) water

3 x 200g (6½-ounce) skinless, boneless salmon fillets

2 cups (400g) medium-grain brown rice

4 eggs, at room temperature

¼ cup (60ml) olive oil

1 medium brown onion (150g), chopped finely

2 cloves garlic, crushed

1 teaspoon finely grated fresh ginger

1½ tablespoons jalfrezi curry paste

2 tablespoons water, extra

1 cup (50g) loosely packed baby spinach

1 fresh long red chilli, sliced thinly

½ cup loosely packed fresh coriander (cilantro)

2 medium limes (180g), cut into wedges

½ cup (140g) Greek-style yoghurt

1 Bring the water to the boil in a medium saucepan over high heat. Add salmon; reduce heat to low, simmer for 5 minutes or until salmon is just cooked. Remove salmon from water; keep warm. Reserve cooking water.

2 Add rice to reserved cooking water; bring to the boil. Reduce heat; simmer, uncovered, for 25 minutes or until tender. (If the rice becomes too dry during cooking, add ½ cup water.)

3 Meanwhile, place eggs in a small saucepan of cold water; bring to the boil. Boil about 7 minutes; drain, rinse under cold running water. Peel eggs; cut in half.

4 Heat 2 tablespoons of the oil in a large, deep frying pan over medium heat; cook onion, stirring occasionally, for 8 minutes or until onion has softened. Add garlic, ginger and paste; cook for 4 minutes or until paste has darkened slightly. Fold through rice with remaining oil, the extra water, spinach, flaked salmon and eggs; cook for 2 minutes or until spinach is wilted and salmon is heated through. Season to taste.

5 Serve kedgeree topped with chilli, coriander and lime wedges; serve with yoghurt.

Jalfrezi curry paste is available from Asian food stores.

Nutritional
COUNT PER SERVING
▶ 44.7g total fat
▶ 10.8g saturated fat
▶ 4163kJ (996 cal)
▶ 84.9g carbohydrate
▶ 60g protein
▶ 5.6g fibre

DRESSINGS

healthy caesar dressing

PREP TIME 5 MINUTES MAKES 1 CUP

Blend or process 1 cup yoghurt, 2 tablespoons olive oil, 2 tablespoons finely grated parmesan, 4 finely chopped anchovies, ½ crushed garlic clove, 1 tablespoon lemon juice and 3 teaspoons dijon mustard until smooth. Season to taste.

TIP Store in a sealed jar in the fridge for up to 1 week.
SERVING SUGGESTION Serve with a caesar salad of cos lettuce, hard-boiled egg, parmesan and crisp bacon or avocado.

maple & dijon dressing

PREP TIME 5 MINUTES MAKES ⅔ CUP

Whisk ¼ cup macadamia oil, ¼ cup apple cider vinegar, 2 tablespoons pure maple syrup and 1 tablespoon dijon mustard in a small bowl until combined. Season to taste.

TIPS Store in a sealed jar in the fridge for up to 1 month. You could substitute olive oil for macadamia oil.
SERVING SUGGESTION Serve with a salad of mixed leaves, or beef and beetroot, or chicken and haloumi, or lamb and roast sweet potato.

raspberry & white balsamic vinaigrette

PREP TIME 5 MINUTES MAKES ½ CUP

Push ½ cup fresh or thawed frozen raspberries through a fine sieve into a small bowl, using the back of a spoon. Whisk in ¼ cup white balsamic vinegar, 2 tablespoons macadamia oil and 1 teaspoon norbu (monk fruit sugar) or stevia granules. Season to taste.

TIP Store in a sealed jar in the fridge for up to 1 week.
SERVING SUGGESTION Serve with a salad of roast duck, slow cooked lamb or grilled chicken.

lemon, avocado & dill dressing

PREP TIME 10 MINUTES MAKES 1½ CUPS

Blend or process 1 medium (250g) avocado, ¼ cup yoghurt, 2 tablespoons avocado oil, ⅓ cup water, ⅓ cup loosely packed fresh dill sprigs and ¼ cup lemon juice until smooth. Season to taste.

TIPS Store in a sealed jar in the fridge for up to 1 week. For a thinner consistency, add a little more water.
SERVING SUGGESTION Serve with a salad of iceberg lettuce and soft-boiled egg, or poached chicken and pistachio, or smoked salmon.

SAUCES

coconut satay sauce

PREP + COOK TIME 10 MINUTES

MAKES 1½ CUPS

Heat 1 tablespoon olive oil in a medium saucepan over medium heat; cook 1 teaspoon finely grated ginger, 1 finely chopped small fresh red chilli and 1 clove crushed garlic for 2 minutes or until fragrant. Add ½ cup crunchy unsalted natural peanut butter, 3 teaspoons soy sauce, 1 teaspoon fish sauce and 1 teaspoon coconut sugar or stevia granules; stir over medium heat. Gradually whisk in 270ml canned coconut cream until combined; cook for 3 minutes or until combined. Stir in 1 tablespoon lime juice.

SERVING SUGGESTION Serve with chicken or beef skewers or gado gado.

honey chilli sauce

PREP + COOK TIME 45 MINUTES

MAKES 1 CUP

Coarsely chop 4 fresh long red chillies. Remove seeds from 12 fresh long red chillies; coarsely chop. Process all chillies with 2 cloves garlic until finely chopped. Transfer to a medium saucepan; add 1¾ cups apple cider vinegar, ¾ cup raw honey and ¼ cup water; cook, stirring, for 5 minutes over low heat until honey melts. Increase heat, bring to a simmer; cook, stirring occasionally, for 20 minutes or until sauce thickens (sauce will thicken further on cooling). Cool.

TIP Store in an airtight container, in the fridge, for up to 1 month.
SERVING SUGGESTION Serve with grilled chicken, prawns, fish, calamari or prawns.

tomato ketchup

PREP + COOK TIME 1 HOUR 15 MINUTES

MAKES 2 CUPS

Heat 1 tablespoon olive oil in a medium saucepan; cook 1 coarsely chopped small brown onion for 5 minutes or until softened. Add 800g (1½ pounds) canned diced tomatoes and ½ cup apple cider vinegar; bring to a boil. Reduce heat to a simmer; stir in 2 tablespoons tomato paste, 2 tablespoons maple syrup, 1 teaspoon sea salt flakes, ½ teaspoon ground cloves, 1 teaspoon ground allspice, ¼ teaspoon cayenne pepper. Simmer over low heat for 1 hour or until sauce reduces and thickens. For a smooth sauce, blend with a stick blender. Cool.

SERVING SUGGESTION **Serve with beef, chicken or lamb burgers and sweet potato fries.**

smoky barbecue sauce

PREP + COOK TIME 35 MINUTES

MAKES 1½ CUPS

Heat 1 tablespoon olive oil in a medium saucepan over medium-high heat; cook 1 finely chopped medium brown onion for 5 minutes or until softened. Add 2 coarsely chopped cloves garlic and 1 tablespoon smoked paprika; cook until fragrant. Add 2 teaspoons finely grated ginger, 1 tablespoon tomato paste, 1 tablespoon dijon mustard, ¼ cup maple syrup, ¼ cup apple cider vinegar and 400g (12½ ounces) canned crushed tomatoes. Simmer, uncovered for 20 minutes or until thickened. Blend sauce until smooth; season to taste. Cool.

SERVING SUGGESTION **Serve with grilled lamb, chicken, beef or pork.**

Dessert

green chilli mango & melon sorbet

PREP + COOK TIME 10 MINUTES (+ FREEZING) SERVES 4

2½ cups (520g) finely chopped mango (see tips)
2½ cups (450g) finely chopped honeydew melon (see tips)
1 fresh long green chilli, seeded, chopped finely
1½ tablespoon finely chopped fresh mint
½ cup fresh micro mint leaves

SUGAR SYRUP
½ cup (125ml) pure fresh apple juice
1 tablespoon finely grated lime rind
2 tablespoons lime juice
⅓ cup (65g) norbu (monk fruit sugar)

1 Place mango and melon in a single layer on a baking-paper-lined tray; sprinkle with chilli. Cover; freeze 5 hours or overnight.

2 Make sugar syrup.

3 Place frozen fruit, chilli and chopped mint in a food processor. With the motor running, slowly pour in sugar syrup until mixture is a smooth sorbet consistency. Tip into a deep freezer-safe tray; freeze 3½ hours, whisking half way through to break up ice crystals.

4 Serve scoops of sorbet in chilled glasses with mint leaves.

SUGAR SYRUP Bring apple juice to the boil in a small saucepan. Reduce heat to medium; simmer until reduced by half. Add rind; cool to room temperature. Whisk in lime juice and norbu until dissolved.

Test Kitchen
NOTES

You will need 3 medium mangoes and ½ medium honeydew melon for the sorbet. Freeze sorbet in an airtight container for up to 2 weeks. You may need to soften the sorbet for 5-10 minutes if it becomes too firm.

Nutritional
COUNT PER SERVING

- 0.5g total fat
- 0.02g saturated fat
- 415kJ (99 cal)
- 19g carbohydrate
- 1.7g protein
- 3.2g fibre

Test Kitchen
NOTES

When blood oranges are out of season use sugar-free blood orange juice (available from most supermarkets) and oranges for the salad. You can use 1½ tablespoons powdered gelatine instead of leaf gelatine. Sprinkle over reduced blood orange juice in step 2; whisk to dissolve. Omit step 3. Jellies can be made the day before and will keep in the fridge for up to 4 days.

blood orange fizzed jelly

PREP + COOK TIME 30 MINUTES (+ STANDING & FREEZING) SERVES 6

The trick to creating these delightful fizzy jellies is to chill the glasses first and set the jellies quickly in the freezer, preserving all the bubbles.

3 cups (750ml) blood orange juice

½ cup (100g) norbu (monk fruit sugar)

2½ leaves titanium-strength gelatine (12.5g)

1¼ cups (310ml) soda water, chilled

2 tablespoon small basil leaves

BLOOD ORANGE SALAD

4 medium blood oranges (680g)

2 pink grapefruit (700g)

100g (3 ounces) strawberries, sliced thickly

1 teaspoon shredded fresh basil leaves

1 teaspoon norbu (monk fruit sugar)

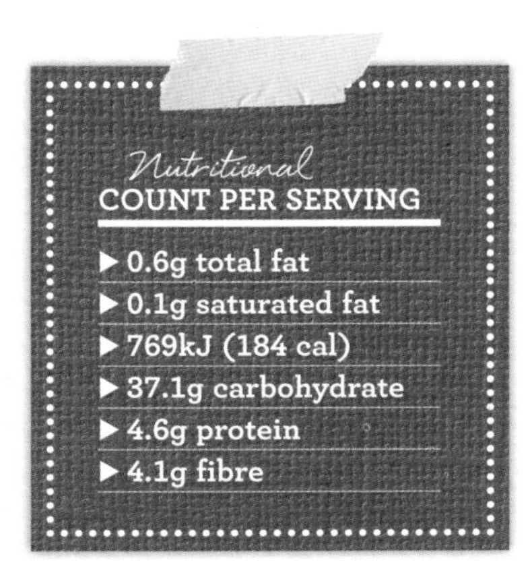

Nutritional COUNT PER SERVING

- 0.6g total fat
- 0.1g saturated fat
- 769kJ (184 cal)
- 37.1g carbohydrate
- 4.6g protein
- 4.1g fibre

1 Chill six ½-cup (125ml) dessert glasses in the freezer.

2 Strain juice into a heavy-based medium saucepan. Add norbu; stir over medium heat until dissolved. Bring to the boil. Reduce heat; simmer, for 15 minutes or until reduced to 1⅔ cups, skimming off any foam.

3 Soak gelatine leaves in cold water for 3 minutes or until softened. Squeeze out excess water, add gelatine to reduced juice; stir until dissolved. Cool to room temperature.

4 Transfer syrup to a large jug. Add soda water, pour into chilled glasses; freeze 1½ hours or until set. (If you are not serving jellies immediately, cover, place in the fridge.)

5 Just before serving, make blood orange salad.

6 Serve jellies topped with blood orange salad and basil.

BLOOD ORANGE SALAD Using a small knife, cut rind with the white pith away from 1 of the oranges. Hold orange over a bowl to catch juices, then cut between the membrane on either side of segments to release the segment into the bowl. Using your hands, squeeze remaining juice from membrane over segments. Repeat with remaining oranges and grapefruit. Add strawberries, basil and norbu to the bowl; stir to combine. Cover; refrigerate until required.

apricot & pistachio frozen yoghurt

PREP + COOK TIME 1 HOUR (+ COOLING & FREEZING) SERVES 4

- **1 cup (150g) dried apricots**
- **2¼ cups (560ml) pure fresh apple juice**
- **1 teaspoon ground cardamom**
- **2¼ cups (630g) Greek-style yoghurt**
- **¼ cup (90g) raw honey**
- **2 tablespoons sesame seeds, toasted**
- **½ cup (70g) pistachios, chopped coarsely**

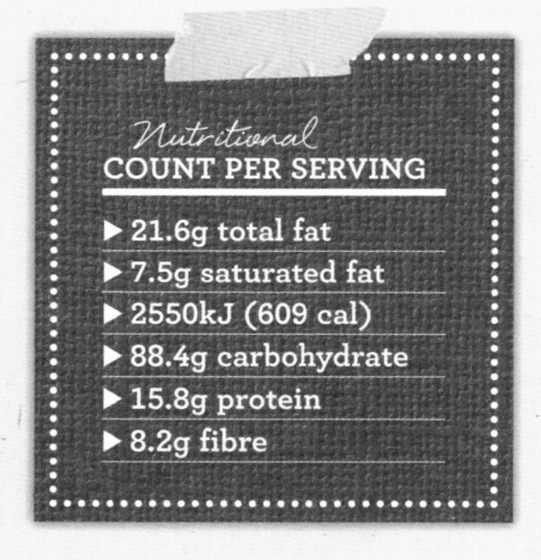

Nutritional
COUNT PER SERVING

- 21.6g total fat
- 7.5g saturated fat
- 2550kJ (609 cal)
- 88.4g carbohydrate
- 15.8g protein
- 8.2g fibre

1 Place apricots and juice in a medium frying pan; bring to the boil. Reduce heat; simmer for 15 minutes or until apricots are tender and plump and the apple juice is syrupy. Cool.

2 Process cooled apricot mixture with cardamom until smooth. Transfer mixture to a large bowl. Cover; refrigerate until required.

3 Combine yoghurt, honey, sesame seeds and half the pistachios in a medium bowl. Place mixture in an ice-cream machine (see tips). Following manufacturer's directions, churn on the frozen yoghurt setting for 40 minutes or until frozen. Spoon frozen yoghurt into bowl with apricot mixture; fold the two mixtures together gently to create a marbled effect. Spoon into a 1.25-litre (5-cup) loaf pan, cover, freeze 5 hours or overnight.

4 Serve yoghurt topped with remaining pistachios.

Test Kitchen NOTES

If you don't have an ice-cream machine, place yoghurt mixture only in the loaf pan, then cover with foil; freeze 1 hour or until half frozen. Pulse mixture in a food processor to break-up ice crystals. Return to pan, cover with foil; repeat freezing and processing. Fold through apricot mixture, return to pan and cover with foil; freeze 5 hours or overnight until frozen. Store yogurt in the freezer for up to 2 weeks.

We used Natvia icing mix made from stevia. It is available in the baking aisle of most supermarkets.

squashed plum & ricotta sandwiches

PREP + COOK TIME 15 MINUTES SERVES 4

- 2 tablespoons melted coconut oil
- 2 teaspoons sugar-free icing mix (see tip)
- 1 teaspoon ground ginger
- 4 medium blood plums (340g), halved, stones removed
- 1 tablespoon pure maple syrup
- 8 x 2cm (¾-inch) slices sourdough bread
- 1 cup (240g) firm ricotta

1 Preheat a sandwich press. Brush press with half the oil.

2 Combine icing mix and ginger in a small bowl.

3 Place plums, cut-side down, in the sandwich press. Cook, pressing down on the lid occasionally, for 6 minutes or until plums are tender and browned. Remove plums; wipe sandwich press clean.

4 Meanwhile, combine maple syrup and remaining oil in a small bowl. Brush oil mixture over one side of each piece of bread.

5 Place four slices of bread, oiled-side down, on a board; spread with ricotta and top with plums. Top with remaining bread slices, oiled-side up. Cook in sandwich press, in two batches, for 3 minutes or until golden and heated through. Serve dusted with ginger mixture.

Nutritional
COUNT PER SERVING

- 17.3g total fat
- 13g saturated fat
- 1565kJ (374 cal)
- 39g carbohydrate
- 13g protein
- 3.9g fibre

Nutritional
COUNT PER SERVING
▶ 26g total fat
▶ 18.8g saturated fat
▶ 3014kJ (520 cal)
▶ 99.4g carbohydrate
▶ 18.4g protein
▶ 4g fibre

buckwheat waffles with grilled peaches

PREP + COOK TIME 15 MINUTES SERVES 4

- ⅓ cup (60g) coconut oil
- 2 tablespoons norbu (monk fruit sugar)
- 3 eggs, separated
- 1 cup (150g) self-raising flour
- ⅓ cup (50g) plain (all-purpose) flour
- ⅓ cup (50g) buckwheat flour
- ⅓ cup (50g) cornflour (cornstarch)
- 1 teaspoon baking powder
- 1 teaspoon bicarbonate of soda (baking soda)
- ½ teaspoon salt
- ½ teaspoon ground ginger
- 1½ cups (375ml) milk
- 1½ teaspoons white vinegar
- cooking-oil spray
- 4 medium yellow peaches (600g), halved, stones removed
- 1 cup (280g) Greek-style yoghurt
- ⅓ cup small fresh mint leaves
- ⅓ cup (90g) raw honey

1 Beat coconut oil and norbu in a medium bowl with an electric mixer until combined. Beat in egg yolks one at a time.
2 Beat egg whites in a small bowl with an electric mixer until soft peaks form. Gently fold egg whites into egg yolk mixture.
3 Fold sifted dry ingredients, milk and vinegar into egg mixture until mixture just comes together (do not over mix; it may look quite lumpy at this stage).
4 Spray a heated waffle iron with cooking oil; pour a level ½-cup of batter on the bottom element of waffle iron. Close iron; cook for 2 minutes or until browned on both sides and crisp. Transfer to a plate; cover to keep warm. Repeat to make 8 waffles in total.
5 Meanwhile, heat an oiled chargrill pan over high heat; cook peaches for 3 minutes each side or until grill marks show.
6 Serve waffles with peaches, yoghurt and mint; drizzle with honey.

rosewater watermelon salad with rosehip syrup

PREP + COOK TIME 40 MINUTES SERVES 4

4 rosehip and hibiscus tea bags
⅔ cup (160ml) hot water
1 tablespoon raw honey
2 tablespoons rosewater
800g (1½ pounds) piece seedless watermelon
4 medium nectarines (480g)
500g (1 pound) strawberries
⅓ cup (45g) pistachios, chopped coarsely
¼ cup loosely packed fresh mint leaves, chopped finely
1 tablespoon small fresh mint leaves, extra

1 Place tea bags in a heatproof jug, cover with the hot water; steep about 30 minutes. Discard tea bags. Place tea with honey in a small heavy-based saucepan, bring to a simmer over medium-high heat; cook for 8 minutes or until reduced to a thick syrup. Remove from heat; stir in rosewater, cool.

2 Meanwhile, remove rind from watermelon and cut flesh into small wedges. Halve and remove stones from nectarines; slice thinly. Halve strawberries.

3 Place chopped fruit in a large bowl with ¼ cup of the pistachios and chopped mint; toss gently to combine. Drizzle with rosehip syrup; serve topped with remaining pistachios and extra mint.

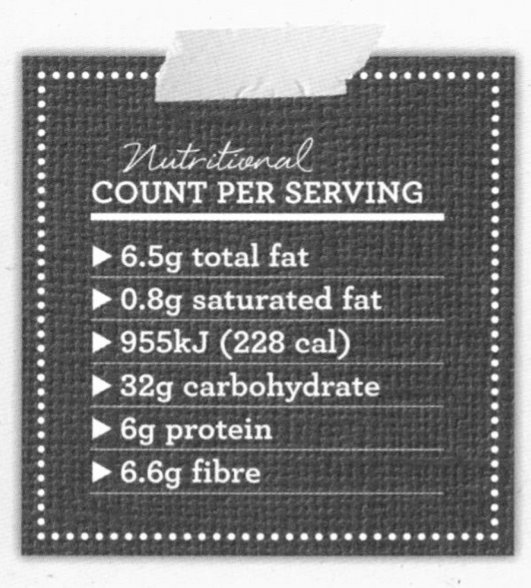

coconut & mango popsicles

PREP + COOK TIME 25 MINUTES (+ FREEZING)
MAKES 8

1¾ cups (265g) frozen diced mango
½ cup (125ml) pure fresh apple juice
2 tablespoons norbu (monk fruit sugar)
¼ cup (60ml) water
270ml coconut cream
½ teaspoon sea salt flakes
8 popsicle sticks
¼ cup (10g) coconut flakes, toasted

1 Process mango and juice until smooth. Place 2 tablespoons mango puree into each of eight ½-cup (125ml) popsicle moulds; freeze 30 minutes.
2 Meanwhile, stir norbu and the water in a small saucepan over low heat until sugar dissolves (do not allow to simmer or boil or the mixture will crystallise). Whisk sugar syrup, coconut cream and salt to combine. Spoon mixture into popsicle moulds to fill. Cover moulds with a double layer of plastic wrap; this will help to keep the popsicle sticks upright. Pierce plastic with a small knife, then push popsicle sticks into each hole. Freeze at least 4 hours or overnight.
3 Dip popsicle moulds briefly in boiling water; remove popsicles. Place coconut flakes in a small bowl, dip each popsicle quickly in hot water then into the coconut. Freeze 10 minutes on a baking-paper-lined tray or until ready to eat.

Nutritional
COUNT PER SERVING
- 8.8g total fat
- 7.8g saturated fat
- 461kJ (110 cal)
- 6.4g carbohydrate
- 0.9g protein
- 0.7g fibre

cacao & date caramel slice

PREP TIME 25 MINUTES (+ REFRIGERATION & FREEZING) MAKES 16

½ cup (115g) fresh dates, pitted
1 cup (130g) roasted almonds
1½ tablespoons coconut oil, melted
¼ teaspoon fine sea salt flakes

DATE CARAMEL

1 cup (230g) fresh dates, pitted
½ cup (125ml) pure maple syrup
⅓ cup (95g) natural crunchy peanut butter
¼ cup (60ml) melted coconut oil

CACAO TOPPING

¼ cup (20g) raw cacao powder
¼ cup (60ml) melted coconut oil
2 teaspoons pure maple syrup

1 Line a 19cm (7¾-inch) square pan with baking paper.
2 Process dates, almonds and oil until smooth. Press mixture evenly onto the base of the pan. Refrigerate 1 hour or until set.
3 Make date caramel; spread mixture evenly over base mixture in pan. Freeze 1 hour or until firm.
4 Make cacao topping. Working quickly, pour topping over date caramel mixture; sprinkle with salt. Refrigerate 1 hour or until set.
5 Use a hot sharp knife to cut slice into 16 pieces.

DATE CARAMEL Process ingredients for 2 minutes or until very smooth.

CACAO TOPPING Whisk ingredients in a medium bowl until smooth.

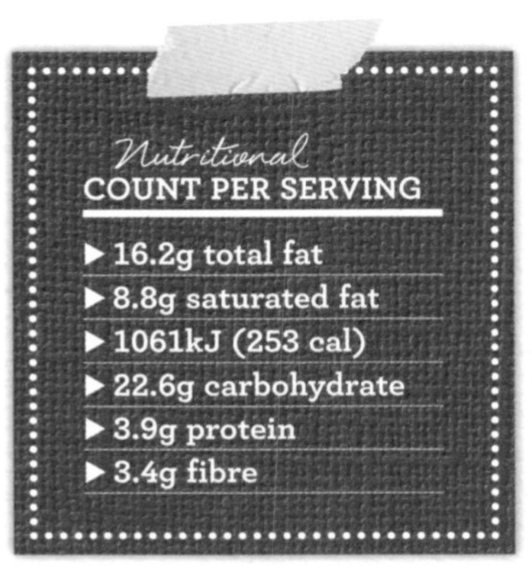

Test Kitchen
NOTES

Make cacao topping just before you are ready to use it or it may begin to set. Slice will keep in an airtight container in the fridge for up to 1 week.

Test Kitchen NOTES

Swap mango or pineapple for berries. Store berry moon rocks in an airtight container for up to 2 weeks.

Nutritional COUNT PER SERVING

- 17.6g total fat
- 5.2g saturated fat
- 1449kJ (346 cal)
- 31.7g carbohydrate
- 11.9g protein
- 5.7g fibre

berry moon rocks

PREP + COOK TIME 15 MINUTES (+ FREEZING) SERVES 4

250g (8 ounces) small strawberries, with stems on
175g (5½ ounces) blackberries
125g (4 ounces) raspberries
400g (12½ ounces) Greek-style yoghurt
1½ tablespoons raw honey
1 vanilla bean, split lengthways, seeds scraped
⅔ cup (90g) finely chopped pistachios

1 Place berries, separated, in a single layer, on a tray; freeze 30 minutes.
2 Combine yoghurt, honey, vanilla seeds and half the pistachios in a medium bowl. Add ½ cup of the frozen raspberries to bowl, crush against the side of bowl with a wooden spoon.
3 Using a toothpick, dip frozen berries, one at a time into yoghurt mixture; place berries on a baking-paper-lined tray. Freeze 3 hours or until coating is set. Cover remaining yoghurt mixture; refrigerate.
4 Repeat dipping coated berries in remaining yoghurt mixture for a second coat; sprinkle with remaining pistachios. Freeze 5 hours or overnight until frozen. Store in an airtight container in the freezer.

Replace the peanuts with any nut you like. Freeze banana treats in an airtight container for up to 3 days.

raw chocolate frozen banana treats

PREP + COOK TIME 15 MINUTES (+ FREEZING) MAKES 24

6 medium bananas (1.2kg)

24 mini popsicle sticks

½ cup (100g) coconut oil, melted

2 tablespoons pure maple syrup

1½ tablespoons raw honey

1 cup (100g) cacao powder

¾ cup (120g) roasted salted peanuts, chopped finely

1 Line two trays with baking paper.

2 Peel and cut bananas into 4cm (1½-inch) pieces; place standing upright on a tray. Push a popsicle stick into each banana piece; freeze 1 hour.

3 Stir oil, maple syrup and honey in a small saucepan over a low heat until almost melted. Remove from heat; continue stirring until completely melted. Sift cacao into coconut oil mixture; whisk until smooth. Transfer to a small jug.

4 Place 1½ teaspoons of the peanuts, apart, in small piles over remaining tray. Dip three-quarters of each banana into cacao mixture; stand upright on a pile of peanuts. Freeze a further 30 minutes or until coating is set.

raw chocolate power puffs

PREP + COOK TIME 20 MINUTES (+ STANDING) MAKES 36

1¼ cups (25g) puffed rice
1¼ cups (40g) puffed millet
½ cup (75g) sunflower seeds
¾ cup (90g) goji berries or unsweetened dried cranberries
¼ cup (35g) chia seeds
½ cup (100g) coconut oil, melted
½ cup (180g) raw honey
1¼ cups (125g) cacao powder

1 Combine puffed rice, puffed millet, sunflower seeds, goji berries and chia seeds in a large bowl.
2 Stir oil and honey in a small saucepan over low heat until almost melted; remove from heat. Add cacao; whisk to combine. Pour cacao mixture over dry ingredients in bowl; stir well to combine.
3 Line an oven tray with baking paper. Using wet hands, roll heaped tablespoons of the mixture into balls, place on tray; refrigerate 30 minutes. Place in an airtight container until ready to eat.

Nutritional
COUNT PER SERVING
- 4.8g total fat
- 2.9g saturated fat
- 335kJ (80 cal)
- 7.4g carbohydrate
- 2g protein
- 0.7g fibre

FRUIT COMPOTES

pear, cardamom & ginger compote

PREP + COOK TIME 45 MINUTES SERVES 4

Place 4 (1kg) cored and thickly sliced packham pears in a medium saucepan with 1 cup water, 2 teaspoons freshly grated ginger, 6 bruised cardamom pods, 1 cinnamon stick and 1 tablespoon lemon juice; bring to the boil. Reduce heat; simmer, partially covered, for 25 minutes, stirring occasionally, or until liquid has reduced slightly and pears are tender. Serve warm or chilled.

SERVING SUGGESTION Serve with vanilla yoghurt or muesli.

plum, raspberry & rosemary compote

PREP + COOK TIME 25 MINUTES SERVES 4

Halve and remove stones from 5 blood plums (450g); cut each half into thirds. Place plums in a large saucepan with ¼ cup water, 1 tablespoon lemon juice, 1 cinnamon stick and 2 sprigs rosemary; bring to the boil. Reduce heat; simmer, covered, about 5 minutes. Uncover; simmer, a further 5 minutes or until plums are just tender. Stir in ½ cup raspberries and 2 teaspoons norbu (monk fruit sugar) or stevia granules until norbu dissolves. Remove from heat.

SERVING SUGGESTION Serve with Greek-style yoghurt.

vanilla-roasted nectarine & peach compote

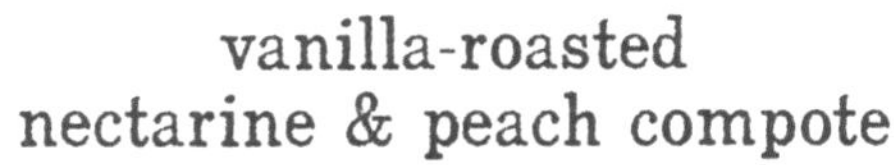

Preheat oven to 220°C/425°F. Grease a medium ovenproof dish with butter. Halve and remove stones from 3 medium (510g) yellow nectarines and 3 medium (450g) yellow peaches; place in dish. Split a vanilla bean lengthways, scrape seeds from halves, using the tip of a knife. Add vanilla bean and seeds to dish with 2 tablespoons pure maple syrup, 2 x 4cm (1½-inch) strips lemon rind, 1 tablespoon lemon juice and a pinch of sea salt flakes; turn fruit to coat. Arrange fruit in a single layer, cut-side up. Bake for 20 minutes or until fruit is tender but still holds its shape. Serve warm or chilled.

SERVING SUGGESTION Serve with thick Greek-style yoghurt topped with nuts and seeds.

apple, rhubarb & goji compote

PREP + COOK TIME 25 MINUTES SERVES 4

Place ½ cup fresh orange juice and 2 tablespoons rice malt syrup in a medium saucepan over low heat; cook, stirring, until syrup melts. Add 2 large (400g) coarsely chopped pink lady apples, 4cm (1½-inch) wide strip of orange rind, the seeds scraped from ½ vanilla bean and the pod; simmer, covered, about 5 minutes. Add 1 bunch (500g) trimmed, coarsely chopped rhubarb and 2 tablespoons goji berries; simmer gently, covered, for 10 minutes or until fruit is tender but still holds its shape. Serve warm or chilled.

TIP Add a crumble topping to make rhubarb and apple crumble.
SERVING SUGGESTION Serve with porridge or yoghurt.

Baking

roasted onion socca with chilli yoghurt

PREP + COOK TIME 40 MINUTES SERVES 8

You will need an ovenproof frying pan for this recipe.

1 medium brown onion (150g)

½ cup (125ml) olive oil

1½ cup (180g) chickpea (besan) flour

1 teaspoon salt flakes

1¼ cup (310ml) lukewarm water

2 teaspoons chopped fresh rosemary

1 tablespoon small fresh rosemary sprigs

¼ cup (20g) finely grated parmesan

CHILLI YOGHURT

½ cup (140g) Greek-style yoghurt

1 teaspoon raw honey

1 tablespoon coarsely chopped fresh flat-leaf parsley

¼ teaspoon chilli flakes

1 Preheat oven to 200°C/400°F. Line an oven tray with baking paper.

2 Cut onion into eight wedges; separate layers. Place onion in a medium bowl with 1 tablespoon of the oil; toss to coat. Season. Place onion on tray; bake for 20 minutes or until browned.

3 Place flour, salt, the lukewarm water, chopped rosemary and ¼ cup of the remaining oil in a medium bowl; whisk until smooth. Season with cracked black pepper. Set aside 5 minutes.

4 Make chilli yoghurt.

5 Increase oven to 250°C/480°F. Heat a large heavy-based ovenproof frying pan over a medium-high heat. Add remaining oil, heat for a few seconds, pour in batter, top with onion and rosemary sprigs. Cook about 1 minute; transfer to oven, bake for 10 minutes or until golden and socca pulls away from the side of the pan.

6 Serve socca cut into wedges, topped with parmesan and chilli yoghurt.

CHILLI YOGHURT Combine ingredients in a small bowl.

Nutritional
COUNT PER SERVING

- 17.6g total fat
- 4.9g saturated fat
- 1048kJ (250 cal)
- 14.7g carbohydrate
- 7.2g protein
- 0.4g fibre

Test Kitchen
NOTES

Socca, also known as farinata, is a traditional Italian and Provençal pancake made from chickpea flour. Reheat socca between sheets of baking paper in a sandwich press. Store socca in an airtight container in the fridge for up to 3 days or freeze for up to 1 month.

seedaholic bread

PREP + COOK TIME 2 HOURS 30 MINUTES (+ STANDING & COOLING) SERVES 2 (MAKES 10 SLICES)

- 1½ cup (135g) rolled oats
- 1½ cups (120g) quinoa flakes
- 1 cup (150g) sunflower seeds
- 1 cup (200g) pepitas (pumpkin seeds)
- ⅔ cup (130g) flax seeds
- ½ cup (70g) white chia seeds
- ½ cup (80g) chopped almond kernels
- ½ cup (70g) chopped hazelnuts
- ½ cup (40g) psyllium husks
- 2 teaspoons sea salt flakes
- 3½ cups (875ml) warm water
- 2 tablespoons raw honey
- ⅔ cup (140g) coconut oil, melted
- ¼ cup (65g) almond butter
- 1 medium packham pear (250g), sliced thinly
- 1 tablespoon olive oil

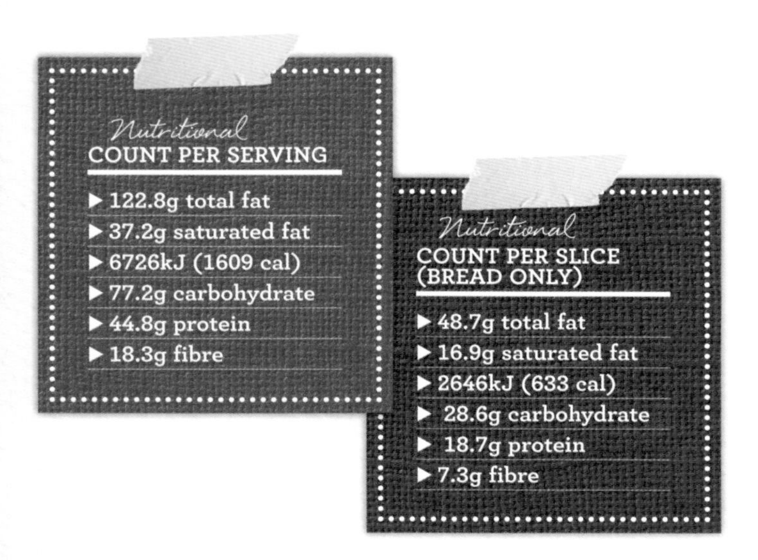

1 Grease a 1.5-litre (6-cup), 14cm x 24cm (5½-inch x 9½-inch) loaf pan; line the base and two long sides with baking paper, extending the paper over the edge.

2 Place dry ingredients in a large bowl. Place the warm water, honey and coconut oil in a large jug; stir until dissolved. Pour over dry ingredients; stir to combine. (The mixture will be firm, if it is too stiff add extra tablespoons of water, one at a time.)

3 Spoon seed mixture into pan; shape with your hands into a loaf shape. Cover surface with plastic wrap; stand at room temperature 2 hours to allow ingredients to absorb the liquid and set the bread into shape.

4 Preheat oven to 200°C/400°F.

5 Bake about 30 minutes. Invert bread onto a wire rack on an oven tray; peel away lining paper. Return bread to oven on tray; bake a further 1 hour 20 minutes (see tips) or until a skewer inserted into the centre comes out clean. Leave 3 hours or until completely cool before slicing.

6 To serve, spread 4 slices of seedaholic bread with almond butter, top with pear slices; drizzle with olive oil. Divide between two serving plates. Season to taste.

Test Kitchen NOTES

Psyllium husks are available from vitamin and health food stores. Position the shelf in the oven so the top of the bread sits in the middle of the oven. If the bread starts to overbrown during baking, cover it loosely with foil. Bread will keep in an airtight container in the fridge for up to 2 weeks. Freeze individual slices in zip-top bags for up to 1 month.

Test Kitchen
NOTES

The even heat provided by the fan function of the oven will help give these scones an extra boost. For conventional ovens, increase the temperature by 10-20 degrees. Scones are best made on day of serving. Jam can be made up to 3 days ahead; store in an airtight container in the fridge for up to 2 weeks or freeze for up to 1 month.

Nutritional
COUNT PER SERVING

- 18.7g total fat
- 10.7g saturated fat
- 1475kJ (352 cal)
- 36g carbohydrate
- 7g protein
- 5.4g fibre

spelt & oat scones with berry chia seed jam

PREP + COOK TIME 50 MINUTES SERVES 8

This jam takes only 10 minutes to make. It won't store as long as regular jam, however it can be frozen in portions to extend the shelf life.

1 cup (150g) wholemeal plain (all-purpose) flour
1 cup (150g) spelt flour
2 teaspoons baking powder
1 teaspoon fine sea salt flakes
100g (3 ounces) cold butter, chopped coarsely
¾ cup (180ml) buttermilk
1 tablespoon raw honey
1 tablespoon buttermilk, extra
2 tablespoons rolled oats
50g (1½ ounces) butter, extra

BERRY CHIA SEED JAM
400g (12½ ounces) frozen mixed berries
¼ cup (35g) white chia seeds
1 tablespoon pure maple syrup
1 teaspoon finely grated lemon rind
1 teaspoon lemon juice
1 vanilla bean, split lengthways, seeds scraped

1 Make berry chia seed jam.
2 Preheat oven to 220°C/425°F fan-forced (see tips). Line an oven tray with baking paper.
3 Sift flours, baking powder and salt into a large bowl; rub in butter until mixture resembles coarse breadcrumbs. Add buttermilk and honey. Using a dinner knife, cut liquid through mixture until it starts to clump. Turn out onto a floured surface; knead gently for 45 seconds or until dough just comes together. (Don't over work the dough or it will be tough.)
4 Shape dough into a 16cm (6½-inch) round on tray with floured hands. Mark the round into eight wedges, using the back of a floured knife. Brush top with extra buttermilk; sprinkle with oats.
5 Bake for 20 minutes or until top is golden. Serve warm with extra butter and jam.

BERRY CHIA SEED JAM Cook berries in a medium saucepan over medium heat, stirring occasionally, for 5 minutes or until berries release their juices. Reduce heat to low, add chia seeds and maple syrup; cook, stirring occasionally, for 6 minutes or until thickened slightly. Stir in rind, juice and vanilla seeds.

glazed fig & whole orange cakes

PREP + COOK TIME 3 HOURS 20 MINUTES (+ STANDING) MAKES 12

- 6 (135g) dried figs, halved
- 1½ cups (375ml) fresh pure apple juice
- 2 medium oranges (480g), washed
- 1⅔ cups (250g) coconut sugar
- 5 eggs
- 2¾ cups (280g) ground almonds
- 1 teaspoon baking powder
- ¼ cup (20g) flaked almonds

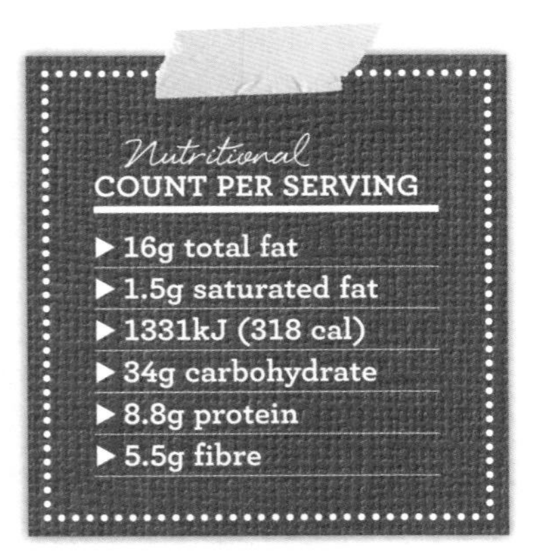

1 Place figs and juice in a medium saucepan; soak 2 hours. Remove figs with a slotted spoon; reserve juice in pan.

2 Meanwhile, fill another medium saucepan two-thirds with water, add whole oranges; bring to the boil. Reduce heat to a simmer. Cover oranges with the lid from a smaller saucepan to keep submerged; simmer about 2 hours, topping up with water if necessary to keep oranges submerged. Drain; cool to room temperature.

3 Preheat oven to 180°C/350°F. Line a 12-hole (⅓-cup/80ml) muffin pan with paper cases.

4 Cut oranges in half, discard any seeds. Process oranges (rind and flesh) until smooth. Add sugar, eggs, ground almonds and baking powder to food processor, pulse until well combined. Spoon mixture into paper cases; place a fig, cut-side up, on top; sprinkle with almonds.

5 Bake for 1 hour or until a skewer inserted in the centre comes out clean.

6 Meanwhile, simmer saucepan with juice over medium heat for 8 minutes or until syrupy.

7 Brush syrup over warm cakes.

Test Kitchen

NOTES

You can use mandarins instead of oranges. If you find the cakes are getting too brown, cover with foil during cooking. Serve topped with Greek-style yoghurt, if you like.

zucchini, parmesan & rosemary crackers

PREP + COOK TIME 30 MINUTES MAKES 35

- 60g (2 ounces) pepitas (pumpkin seeds)
- ½ cup (55g) coarsely chopped walnuts
- 1 small zucchini (90g), chopped coarsely
- ⅓ cup (25g) finely grated parmesan
- 1 tablespoon linseeds (flaxseeds)
- 1 tablespoon sesame seeds
- 1 tablespoon poppy seeds
- ½ teaspoon cumin seeds
- ½ teaspoon dried oregano
- 1 teaspoon finely chopped fresh rosemary
- 1 tablespoon fresh rosemary leaves
- ½ teaspoon sea salt flakes

1 Preheat oven to 180°C/350°F.

2 Process pepitas and walnuts until finely ground. Add zucchini; process to combine. Add parmesan, seeds, oregano and chopped rosemary; pulse to combine. Season.

3 Spread mixture onto a piece of baking paper; top with a second sheet of baking paper. Roll into a 25cm x 35cm (10-inch x 14-inch) rectangle about 2mm (⅛-inch) thick. Transfer cracker on paper to a large oven tray; remove top sheet of baking paper.

4 Using a knife, score dough at 5cm (2-inch) intervals crossways then lengthways to mark out 5cm (2-inch) squares. Sprinkle with rosemary leaves and sea salt.

5 Bake for 20 minutes, rotating tray halfway through cooking, or until golden. (Cover with foil if it starts to overbrown.) Cool on tray. Break into pieces along marked lines before serving.

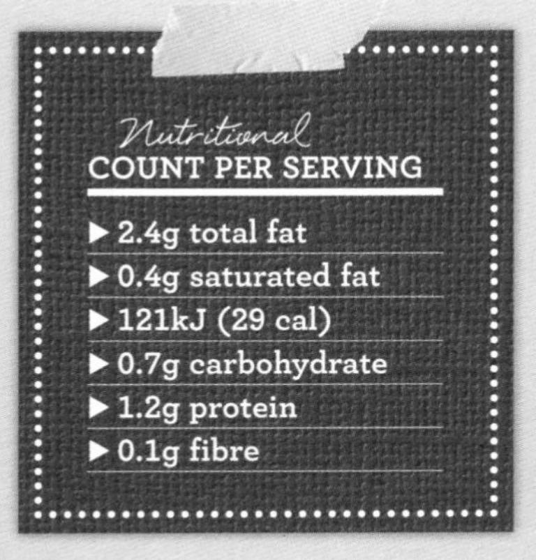

Crackers will keep in an airtight container for up to 5 days.

peach & pistachio cake pots

PREP + COOK TIME 45 MINUTES MAKES 12

- 4 small peaches (460g), halved
- 1 cup (280g) Greek-style yoghurt
- 2 medium apples (300g), grated coarsely
- 2 eggs, beaten lightly
- ¼ cup (60ml) milk
- 2 tablespoons raw honey
- 2 cups (240g) ground almonds
- 2 teaspoons baking powder
- ⅓ cup (45g) pistachios, chopped coarsely
- 1½ tablespoons raw honey, extra

1 Preheat oven to 180°C/350°F. Cut 12 x 12cm (4-inch) squares of baking paper; line 12 (⅓-cup/80ml) ovenproof pots with paper squares (see tips).

2 Thinly slice three of the peaches. Coarsely chop remaining peach; blend or process to a coarse puree. Fold peach puree through yoghurt in a small bowl; cover and refrigerate until required.

3 Place apple, egg, milk, honey, ground almonds and baking powder in a large bowl; mix until just combined. Divide mixture between pots; push peach slices 2cm (¾-inch) into the top of the batter.

4 Bake for 30 minutes or until a skewer inserted in the centre comes out clean.

5 Top cakes with pistachios; drizzle with extra honey. Serve warm or at room temperature with peach yoghurt.

Test Kitchen

NOTES

We used peat seedling pots available from hardware stores and garden nurseries. You can also cook the cakes in a 12-hole (⅓-cup/80ml) muffin pan, lined with baking paper squares. This recipe is best made on day of serving.

apple & spice free-form tarts

PREP + COOK TIME 1 HOUR 20 MINUTES (+ REFRIGERATION) MAKES 6

4 large green apples (800g), peeled, cored, sliced thickly
⅔ cup (90g) coconut sugar, plus extra to dust
¼ cup (40g) spelt flour
1 teaspoon ground cinnamon
½ teaspoon ground ginger
1 teaspoon ground cardamom
½ teaspoon sea salt flakes
30g (1 ounce) butter, chopped finely
2 tablespoons apple cider vinegar
1 cup (280g) Greek-style yoghurt
1 teaspoon finely grated orange rind

SPELT PASTRY

3 cups (390g) spelt flour
1 vanilla bean, split lengthways, seeds scraped
¼ cup (40g) coconut sugar
½ teaspoon ground nutmeg
½ teaspoon sea salt flakes
200g (6½ ounces) butter, cut into small cubes
2 tablespoons iced water, approximately

1 Make pastry.
2 Place apples, sugar, flour, spices, salt, butter and vinegar in a large bowl; toss to coat.
3 Preheat oven to 180°C/350°F. Line two oven trays with baking paper.
4 Cut pastry in half; roll out each piece between two sheets of lightly floured baking paper until 3mm (⅛-inch) thick. Remove top layer of paper. Using a 17cm (6¾-inch) bowl (or plate) as a guide, cut out 3 rounds from each pastry half. Place apple mixture in the centre, leaving a 3cm (1¼-inch) border. Reserve liquid from apple in the bowl. Fold pastry in, pleating it as you go to partially overlap the filling and create an open-topped pie.
5 Transfer pies to trays, brush with liquid from apple mixture; bake for 50 minutes or until golden and apples are tender.
6 Meanwhile, combine yoghurt and rind in a small bowl.
7 Using a large metal lifter, carefully transfer pies to plates. Serve with orange yoghurt.

SPELT PASTRY Process flour, vanilla seeds, sugar, nutmeg, salt and butter until mixture resembles crumbs. Add the iced water; pulse until mixture just forms a dough. Shape into a disc, wrap in plastic wrap; refrigerate 1 hour.

Nutritional
COUNT PER SERVING

- 35g total fat
- 22g saturated fat
- 3093kJ (739 cal)
- 94g carbohydrate
- 11.8g protein
- 2.7g fibre

apricot & hazelnut crumble

PREP + COOK TIME 1 HOUR SERVES 4

- **4 medium apricots (325g)**
- **2 medium pears (460g)**
- **80g (2½ ounces) dried figs**
- **10g (½ ounce) butter**
- **¾ cup (180ml) water**
- **½ cup (125ml) pure maple syrup**
- **¾ cup (60g) quinoa flakes**
- **¼ cup (30g) ground hazelnuts**
- **½ cup (70g) coarsely chopped skinless hazelnuts, roasted**
- **½ teaspoon sea salt flakes**
- **1 cup (280g) Greek-style yoghurt**
- **2 teaspoons long thin strips orange rind**

1 Preheat oven to 180°C/350°F.

2 Cut apricots in half; remove and discard stones. Cut unpeeled pears in half; remove core and cut each half into three wedges. Remove stem end from figs and quarter.

3 Combine apricot, pear, fig, butter and the water in a medium saucepan over medium heat; cook, stirring occasionally, for 6 minutes or until pears have softened slightly. Transfer fruit mixture to a 1.5 litre (6-cup) ovenproof dish.

4 Combine maple syrup, quinoa flakes, ground hazelnuts, chopped hazelnuts and salt in a medium bowl; sprinkle over fruit.

5 Bake for 45 minutes or until top is lightly golden. Serve warm topped with yoghurt and rind.

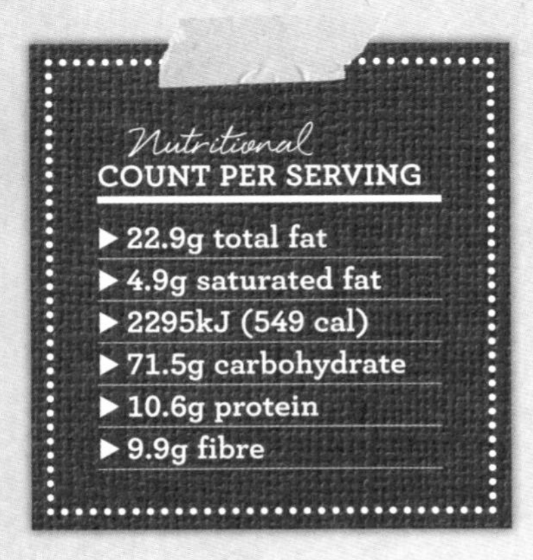

Test Kitchen
NOTES

You can swap 3 peaches for the pears, ground almonds for the ground hazelnuts, coarsely chopped almonds for the hazelnuts and raw honey for the maple syrup.

caramelised onion & kumara tarte tartin

PREP + COOK TIME 2 HOURS (+ REFRIGERATION) SERVES 6

- 20g (¾ ounce) butter
- 1 tablespoon olive oil
- 1 tablespoon pure maple syrup
- 3 cloves garlic, sliced thinly
- ½ teaspoon ground nutmeg
- 1 tablespoon fresh lemon thyme leaves
- 350g (11 ounces) baby kumara (orange sweet potato), cut into 1cm (½-inch) slices
- 1 cup (250ml) water
- 2 sheets puff pastry
- 1 egg yolk
- 1 tablespoon milk or water
- 100g (3 ounces) goat's curd

CARAMELISED ONIONS

- 20g (¾ ounce) butter
- 1 tablespoon olive oil
- 4 medium onions (800g), sliced finely
- ¼ cup (60ml) balsamic vinegar
- 2 tablespoons pure maple syrup
- 1 tablespoon dijon mustard

Nutritional **COUNT PER SERVING**

- 25g total fat
- 10.7g saturated fat
- 1910kJ (456 cal)
- 49.6g carbohydrate
- 9.3g protein
- 5.2g fibre

1 Make caramelised onions.

2 Heat butter, oil and maple syrup in a 30cm (12-inch) ovenproof frying pan over medium heat. Add garlic; cook, stirring, about 1 minute. Remove pan from heat. Sprinkle nutmeg and thyme over base of pan; pack kumara slices, in a single layer, on top; season. Pour half the water over kumara. Return pan to heat; cook for 8 minutes or until the water evaporates. Add remaining water; cook a further 8 minutes or until kumara are browned underneath. Remove from heat; cool 5 minutes.

3 Spoon caramelised onions evenly over kumara with the back of a spoon. Set aside in the fridge to cool completely.

4 Preheat oven to 200°C/400°F.

5 Cut each pasty sheet on a diagonal into two triangles. Whisk egg yolk and milk together in a small bowl. Make a larger square with the four triangles, with the longest edges of the triangles forming the outside of the square; use a little egg wash to stick the pastry together. Place the pastry over the tart and trim overhang. Fold, nip and tuck the edges in to form the pastry around the tart. Brush with egg mixture and prick lightly with a fork. Bake for 20 minutes or until crisp and golden. Stand tart in pan 5 minutes.

6 To serve, place pan over medium heat about 30 seconds to loosen the base then invert onto a wooden board, top with spoonfuls of goat's curd and sprinkle with extra lemon thyme, if you like.

CARAMELISED ONIONS Heat butter and oil in a large heavy-based frying pan over medium heat; cook onion, stirring frequently for 30 minutes or until very soft and golden. Add vinegar, maple syrup and mustard; cook for 30 minutes over low heat or until caramelised and reduced. Season.

zucchini & blueberry loaf cakes

PREP + COOK TIME 45 MINUTES MAKES 8

- 3 medium zucchini (360g), grated coarsely
- 2¾ cups (300g) ground almonds
- ¾ cup (120g) coconut sugar
- 1 teaspoon ground cinnamon
- ½ teaspoon sea salt
- 2 teaspoons baking powder
- ½ cup (175g) pure maple syrup
- ½ cup (125ml) melted virgin coconut oil
- 3 eggs, beaten lightly
- 1 vanilla bean, split lengthways, seeds scraped
- 2 teaspoons finely grated orange rind
- ⅓ cup (80ml) orange juice
- 1 cup (150g) frozen blueberries
- ½ cup (25g) coconut flakes, toasted

1 Preheat oven to 180°C/350°F. Grease an 8-hole (½-cup/125ml) loaf pan tray; line base and long sides of holes with strips of baking paper, extending the paper 3cm (1¼-inches) over long sides.
2 Squeeze liquid from zucchini; place zucchini in a large bowl. Add ground almonds, sugar, cinnamon, salt and baking powder; stir to combine.
3 Whisk maple syrup, oil, egg, vanilla seeds, rind and juice in a small bowl. Add syrup mixture to zucchini mixture; stir gently to combine. Fold in blueberries. Spoon mixture into pan holes.
4 Bake for 30 minutes or until risen and slightly cracked on top. Leave loaves in pan 5 minutes before turning, top-side up, onto a wire rack to cool.
5 Brush loaves with a little extra maple syrup; sprinkle with toasted coconut.

Nutritional
COUNT PER SERVING

- 39.2g total fat
- 16.3g saturated fat
- 2227kJ (532 cal)
- 34.5g carbohydrate
- 10.7g protein
- 4.4g fibre

Test Kitchen
NOTES

You can use any nut meal in this gluten-free recipe. Swap the blueberries for raspberries for a more tart taste. Cakes will keep in an airtight container for up to 3 days or in the freezer for up to 1 month.

MUFFINS

coconut & vanilla muffins

PREP + COOK TIME 40 MINUTES MAKES 12

Preheat oven to 180°C/350°F. Line a 12-hole (⅓-cup/80ml) muffin pan with paper cases. Sift 2 cups spelt flour and 2 teaspoons baking powder into a medium bowl. Whisk 1 teaspoon vanilla extract (see tip), 1 cup yoghurt, ½ cup melted cooled virgin coconut oil, ½ cup pure maple syrup and 2 eggs in a medium jug. Pour over dry ingredients; stir with a fork to just combine. Spoon mixture into cases; top with 1 cup coconut flakes. Bake for 30 minutes or until a skewer inserted into the centre comes out clean.

TIP Vanilla extract contains a tiny amount of refined sugar; if you prefer, either use the scraped seeds of a vanilla bean or vanilla bean powder available from health food stores.

peach & ginger crumble muffins

PREP + COOK TIME 40 MINUTES MAKES 12

Preheat oven to 180°C/350°F. Line a 12-hole (⅓-cup/80ml) muffin pan with paper cases. Sift 2 cups spelt flour, 2 teaspoons baking powder, 1½ teaspoons ground ginger and 1 teaspoon ground cinnamon into a medium bowl; stir in 2 (250g) coarsely chopped small peaches. Whisk 1 teaspoon vanilla extract (see previous tip), 1 cup yoghurt, ½ cup melted cooled virgin coconut oil, ½ cup pure maple syrup and 2 eggs in a medium jug. Pour over dry ingredients; stir with a fork to just combine. Spoon mixture into cases. Place ⅓ cup coconut sugar, ½ cup spelt flour and 1 teaspoon ground cinnamon in a small bowl; rub in 60g (2 ounces) chopped cold unsalted butter until mixture resembles coarse crumbs. Sprinkle crumble on muffins. Bake for 30 minutes or until a skewer inserted into the centre comes out clean.

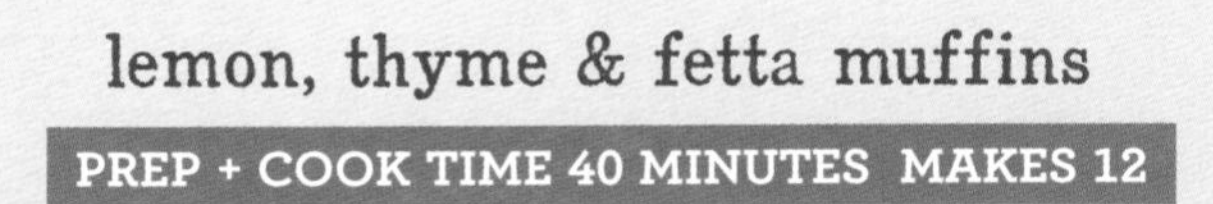

lemon, thyme & fetta muffins

PREP + COOK TIME 40 MINUTES MAKES 12

Preheat oven to 180°C/350°F. Line a 12-hole (⅓-cup/80ml) muffin pan with paper cases. Sift 2 cups spelt flour and 2 teaspoons baking powder into a medium bowl; stir in 2 teaspoons finely grated lemon rind and 1 tablespoon finely chopped fresh thyme. Whisk 1¼ cups yoghurt, ½ cup melted cooled virgin coconut oil, ¼ cup pure maple syrup and 2 eggs in a medium jug. Pour over dry ingredients; stir with a fork until almost combined. Fold through ½ cup crumbled goat's fetta. Spoon mixture into cases; top with combined ⅔ cup crumbled goat's fetta, ⅓ cup pepitas and 2 tablespoons fresh thyme leaves. Bake for 30 minutes or until a skewer inserted into the centre comes out clean.

choc, beetroot & walnut muffins

PREP + COOK TIME 40 MINUTES MAKES 12

Preheat oven to 180°C/350°F. Line a 12-hole (⅓-cup/80ml) muffin pan with paper cases. Sift 2 cups spelt flour, ⅓ cup cacao powder and 2½ teaspoons baking powder into a medium bowl. Coarsely grate 1 medium (130g) washed, unpeeled beetroot, place in a large jug. Add 1½ cups yoghurt, ½ cup melted cooled virgin coconut oil, ½ cup pure maple syrup and 2 eggs to the jug; whisk with a fork to combine. Pour over dry ingredients; stir with the fork until almost combined. Fold in 8 pitted and coarsely chopped fresh medjool dates and ½ cup chopped roasted walnuts. Spoon mixture into cases. Bake for 30 minutes or until a skewer inserted into the centre comes out clean.

Cooking TECHNIQUES

trimming beetroot

Cut the stems of beetroot to 2cm (¾ inch) from the bulb. Don't trim the beard at the base of the plant as this stops the colour from bleeding during cooking.

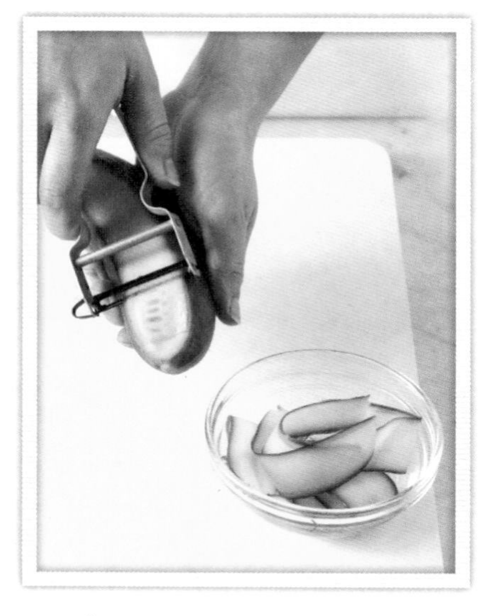

slicing vegies thinly

Cutting cucumber, zucchini, carrots, etc. into thin ribbons gives long thin, uniform slices. Use a vegetable peeler to do this. Applying more pressure on the peeler gives a thicker slice.

washing a leek

Cut the leek in half lengthwise, stopping at the root. Fan the layers out and wash under fast-running cold water. This removes any grit from the inside layers.

slicing fennel

Use a V-slicer or mandoline – simply slide the fennel back and forth across the blade. The adjustable blade is very sharp, so watch your fingers. A guard is supplied, so use it to protect your fingers from any unwanted mishaps.

seeding a pomegranate

Cut the pomegranate in half and hold it over a bowl. Hit it sharply with a spoon - the seeds (surrounded by the pulp) should fall out - if they don't, dig them out with a teaspoon. Be careful, as pomegranate juice can stain your hands, clothes and bench top.

cutting onion wedges

Cut the onion in half lengthways through the root. Remove the papery outer skin. Lie the onion cut-side down and cut lengthways through the root into triangular-shaped wedges. The root holds the wedges together.

slicing capsicum

Cut the top and bottom off and stand capsicum on one end; slice down removing all the flesh. Remove and discard the seeds and membranes, then slice the flesh.

zesting citrus fruit

A zester has very small and very sharp holes that cut the rind (the outermost layer of the fruit) into thin ribbons but leaves the bitter pith (the white layer) behind.

making a thin omelette

Lightly whisk eggs then pour into a heated lightly-oiled wok (or large frying pan). Tilt the wok to cover the base with the egg; cook until the egg is set.

how to chiffonade

Chiffonade is a way of cutting green leaves into long, thin strips. Lay leaves flat on top of each other, then roll up tightly and cut into thin slices.

toasting nuts

Add nuts to a small dry frying pan; cook, stirring occasionally, over medium heat for 4 minutes or until golden. Remove from pan; cool.

crushing garlic

Press garlic firmly with the flat blade of a large knife (top) crushing the clove. Simply pull off the papery skin. A garlic press (bottom) removes and leaves the skin behind while crushing the garlic.

GLOSSARY

AGAVE SYRUP (ah-GAH-vay) also known as agave nectar; a sweetener produced from the agave plant in South Africa and Mexico (a succulent with thick fleshy leaves, each ending generally in a sharp point and having spiny edges; it is the plant from which tequila is made).

ALLSPICE also known as pimento or jamaican pepper; so-named because it tastes like a combination of nutmeg, cumin, clove and cinnamon. Available whole or ground.

ALMONDS

ground also called almond meal; almonds are powdered to a coarse flour-like texture.

flaked paper-thin slices.

BAKING PAPER also called parchment paper or baking parchment; a silicone-coated paper that is primarily used for lining baking pans and oven trays so cooked food doesn't stick.

BEETROOT (BEETS) also known as red beets; firm, round root vegetable.

BICARBONATE OF SODA (BAKING SODA) a raising agent.

BUTTER use salted or unsalted (sweet) butter; 125g is equal to one stick of butter (4 ounces).

BUTTERMILK originally the term given to the slightly sour liquid left after butter was churned from cream, today it is made from no-fat or low-fat milk to which specific bacterial cultures have been added. Despite its name, it is actually low in fat.

CACAO

beans contained inside the large cacao pod. The beans are used to make cocoa butter, cocoa powder, cocoa solids and chocolate.

cacao (cocoa) butter rich in saturated fats; about a third is stearic acid, but this acts differently to other saturated fats in that it doesn't raise cholesterol and, in fact, lowers LDL (bad) cholesterol.

dutch-processed cacao powder treated with an alkali to neutralize its acidity; it is darker and more mellow in flavour.

nibs can be separated into cocoa butter and powder. Cocoa powder retains many beneficial antioxidants and is an easy way of adding cocoa into your diet without the kilojoules of chocolate.

raw cacao powder made by removing the cocoa butter using a process known as cold-pressing. It retains more of its nutrients than heat-processed cacao powder; it also has a stronger, slightly bitter, taste.

raw dark chocolate made using cold-pressed raw cacao beans, that is, without the use of heat. It is high in antioxidants, and has good levels of chromium, iron and magnesium, which support healthy heart function.

CAPSICUM (BELL PEPPER) also known as bell pepper or, simply, pepper. Native to Central and South America, they can be red, green, yellow, orange or purplish-black in colour. Be sure to discard seeds and membranes before use.

CARDAMOM a spice native to India and used extensively in its cuisine; can be purchased in pod, seed or ground form. Has a distinctive aromatic, sweetly rich flavour.

CHEESE

fetta Greek in origin; a crumbly textured goat- or sheep-milk cheese having a sharp, salty taste. Ripened and stored in salted whey; particularly good cubed and tossed into salads.

fetta, persian a soft, creamy fetta marinated in a blend of olive oil, garlic, herbs and spices. It is available from most larger supermarkets.

goat's made from goat's milk, has an earthy, strong taste; available in both soft and firm textures, in various shapes and sizes, and sometimes rolled in ash or herbs.

haloumi a firm, cream-coloured sheep-milk cheese matured in brine; haloumi can be grilled or fried, briefly, without breaking down. Should be eaten while still warm as it becomes tough and rubbery on cooling.

mozzarella soft, spun-curd cheese; originating in southern Italy where it was traditionally made from water-buffalo milk. The most popular pizza cheese because of its low melting point and elasticity when heated.

parmesan also called parmigiano; a hard, grainy cow-milk cheese originating in Italy. Reggiano is the best variety.

pecorino the Italian generic name for cheeses made from sheep milk; hard, white to pale-yellow cheeses. If you can't find it, use parmesan.

ricotta a soft, sweet, moist, white cow-milk cheese with a low fat content and a slightly grainy texture. The name roughly translates as 'cooked again' and refers to ricotta's manufacture from a whey that is itself a by-product of other cheese making.

CHICKPEAS (GARBANZO BEANS) an irregularly round, sandy-coloured legume. Has a firm texture even after cooking, a floury mouth-feel and robust nutty flavour; available canned or dried (reconstitute for several hours in cold water before use).

CHILLI available in many different types and sizes. Use rubber gloves when seeding and chopping fresh chillies as they can burn your skin. Removing seeds and membranes lessens the heat level.

cayenne pepper a long, thin-fleshed, extremely hot red chilli usually sold dried and ground.

green any unripened chilli; also some particular varieties that are ripe when green, such as jalapeño, habanero, poblano or serrano.

long available both fresh and dried; a generic term used for any moderately hot, thin, long (6-8cm/2¼-3¼ inch) chilli.

red thai also known as 'scuds'; small, very hot and bright red; can be substituted with fresh serrano or habanero chillies.

CHINESE COOKING WINE (SHAO HSING) also known as chinese rice wine; made from fermented rice, wheat, sugar and salt with a 13.5% alcohol content. Inexpensive and found in Asian food shops; if you can't find it, replace with mirin or sherry.

CINNAMON available in sticks (quills) and ground into powder; used as a sweet, fragrant flavouring in sweet and savoury foods.

COCOA POWDER also known as cocoa; dried, unsweetened, roasted and ground cocoa beans (cacao seeds).

COCONUT

cream comes from the first pressing of the coconut flesh, without the addition of water; the second pressing (less rich) is sold as coconut milk. Look for coconut cream labelled as 100% coconut, without added emulsifiers.

flaked dried flaked coconut flesh.

milk not the liquid found inside the fruit (coconut water), but the diluted liquid from the second pressing of the white flesh of a mature coconut (the first pressing produces coconut cream).

shredded thin strips of dried coconut.

sugar not made from coconuts, but from the sap of the blossoms of the coconut palm tree. The refined sap looks a little like raw or light brown sugar, and has a similar caramel flavour. It has the same amount of kilojoules as regular table (white) sugar.

water the liquid from the centre of a young green coconut. It has fewer kilojoules than fruit juice, with no fat or protein. There are sugars present, but these are slowly absorbed giving coconut water a low GI.

young coconuts that are not fully mature. As a coconut ages, the amount of juice inside decreases, until it disappears and is replaced by air.

CORIANDER (CILANTRO) a bright-green leafy herb with a pungent flavour. Both the stems and roots of coriander are used in cooking; wash well before using. Also available ground or as seeds; these should not be substituted for fresh coriander as the tastes are completely different.

CREAM we use fresh cream, also known as pure cream and pouring cream, unless otherwise stated; it has no additives unlike commercially thickened cream.

CRÈME FRAÎCHE a mature, naturally fermented cream (minimum fat content of 35%) having a velvety texture and slightly tangy, nutty flavour. Crème fraîche, a French variation of sour cream, can boil without curdling and be used in sweet and savoury dishes.

CUMIN also known as zeera or comino; has a spicy, nutty flavour.

DATES fruit of the date palm tree, eaten fresh or dried. About 4cm to 6cm in length, oval and plump, thin-skinned, with a honey-sweet flavour and sticky texture.

FENNEL also known as finocchio or anise; a white to very pale green-white, firm, crisp, roundish vegetable about 8-12cm in diameter. The bulb has a slightly sweet, anise flavour but the leaves have a much stronger taste. Also the name given to dried seeds having a licorice flavour.

FIGS best eaten in peak season, at the height of summer. Figs are also glacéd (candied), dried or canned in sugar syrup; these are usually sold at health food stores, Middle Eastern food shops or specialty cheese counters.

FISH SAUCE called naam pla (if Thai made) and nuoc naam (if Vietnamese); the two are almost identical. Made from pulverised salted fermented fish (often anchovies); has a pungent smell and strong taste. Available in varying degrees of intensity, so use according to your taste.

FLOUR

buckwheat a herb in the same plant family as rhubarb; not a cereal so it is gluten-free.

chickpea (besan) made from ground chickpeas so is gluten-free and high in protein. Used in Indian cooking.

coconut a low carbohydrate, high fibre, gluten-free flour made from fresh dried coconut flesh. It has a sweetish taste and is suitable for those on a paleo diet.

plain (all-purpose) an all-purpose wheat flour.

self-raising plain flour sifted with baking powder in the proportion of 1 cup flour to 2 teaspoons baking powder.

wholemeal also known as wholewheat flour; milled with the wheat germ so is higher in fibre and more nutritional than plain flour.

GINGER also known as green or root ginger; the thick root of a tropical plant.

ground also known as powdered ginger; cannot be substituted for fresh ginger.

GOJI BERRIES (DRIED) small, very juicy, sweet red berries that grow on a type of shrub in Tibet. Believed to be high in nutrients and antioxidants.

KAFFIR LIME LEAVES also known as bai magrood. Aromatic leaves of a citrus tree; two glossy dark green leaves joined end to end, forming a rounded hourglass shape. A strip of fresh lime peel may be substituted for each kaffir lime leaf.

KUMARA (ORANGE SWEET POTATO) the Polynesian name of an orange-fleshed sweet potato often confused with yam.

LABNE a soft cheese made by salting plain (natural) yoghurt and draining it of whey for up to 2 days until it becomes thick enough to roll into small balls, which may be sprinkled with or rolled in chopped herbs or spices.

LEEKS a member of the onion family, the leek resembles a green onion but is much larger and more subtle in flavour. Tender baby or pencil leeks can be eaten whole with minimal cooking but adult leeks are usually trimmed of most of the green tops then sliced.

MAPLE SYRUP, PURE distilled from the sap of sugar maple trees found only in Canada and the USA.

MUSHROOMS

button small, cultivated white mushrooms with a mild flavour. When a recipe calls for an unspecified type of mushroom, use button.

fresh shiitake also called chinese black, forest or golden oak mushrooms; although cultivated, they are large and meaty and have the earthiness and taste of wild mushrooms.

MUSLIN inexpensive, undyed, finely woven cotton fabric called for in cooking to strain stocks and sauces.

NOODLES, UDON available fresh and dried, these broad, white, wheat Japanese noodles are similar to those in home-made chicken noodle soup.

NORI a type of dried seaweed used as a flavouring, garnish and in sushi. Sold in thin sheets, plain or toasted (yaki-nori).

OIL

coconut extracted from the coconut flesh so you don't get any of the fibre, protein or carbohydrates present in the whole coconut. The best quality is virgin coconut oil, which is the oil pressed from the dried coconut flesh and doesn't include the use of solvents or other refining processes.

cooking spray we use a canola oil cooking spray.

olive made from ripened olives. Extra virgin and virgin are the first and second press, respectively, of the olives and are therefore considered the best; the "extra light" or "light" name on other types refers to taste not fat levels.

peanut pressed from ground peanuts; used in Asian cooking because of its capacity to handle heat without burning.

sesame made from roasted, crushed, white sesame seeds; a flavouring rather than a cooking medium.

vegetable oils sourced from plant rather than animal fats.

ONIONS, GREEN (SCALLIONS) also known, incorrectly, as shallot; an immature onion picked before the bulb has formed. Has a long, bright-green edible stalk.

PEPITAS (PUMPKIN SEEDS) the pale green kernels of dried pumpkin seeds; they can be bought plain or salted.

POMEGRANATES dark-red, leathery-skinned fresh fruit about the size of an orange filled with hundreds of seeds, each wrapped in an edible lucent-crimson pulp having a unique tangy sweet-sour flavour.

POPPY SEEDS small, dried, bluish-grey seeds of the poppy plant, with a crunchy texture and a nutty flavour. Can be purchased whole or ground in delicatessens and most supermarkets.

QUINOA (KEEN-WA) a gluten-free grain. It has a delicate, slightly nutty taste and chewy texture. Always rinse well before use.

ROASTING/TOASTING desiccated coconut, pine nuts and sesame seeds roast more evenly if stirred over low heat in a heavy-based frying pan; their natural oils will help turn them golden brown. Remove from pan immediately. Nuts and dried coconut can be roasted in the oven to release their aromatic essential oils. Spread evenly onto an oven tray then roast at 180°C/350°F for about 5 minutes.

SILVER BEET also known as swiss chard; mistakenly called spinach.

SOY SAUCE made from fermented soy beans. Several variations are available in most supermarkets and Asian food stores. We use japanese soy sauce unless otherwise indicated.

SPINACH also known as english spinach and, incorrectly, silver beet. Baby spinach leaves are best eaten raw in salads; the larger leaves should be added last to soups, stews and stir-fries, and should be cooked until barely wilted.

TAHINI a rich, sesame-seed paste, used in most Middle-Eastern cuisines, especially Lebanese, dips and sauces.

TAMARIND the tamarind tree produces clusters of hairy brown pods, each of which is filled with seeds and a viscous pulp, that are dried and pressed into the blocks of tamarind found in Asian food shops. Gives a sweet-sour, slightly astringent taste to marinades, sauces and dressings.

VANILLA

bean dried, long, thin pod from a tropical golden orchid; the minuscule black seeds inside the bean impart a luscious flavour in baking and desserts.

extract obtained from vanilla beans infused in water; a non-alcoholic version of essence. Vanilla extract contains a tiny amount of refined sugar; if you prefer, either use the scraped seeds of a vanilla bean or vanilla bean powder available from health food stores

WALNUTS the shell of the ripe nut is creamy brown with a striated surface; the kernel is ridged and oval and formed in two distinct halves.

WATERCRESS one of the cress family, a large group of peppery greens. Highly perishable, so must be used as soon as possible after purchase. It has an exceptionally high vitamin K content.

YOGHURT we use plain full-cream yoghurt unless noted otherwise.

Greek-style plain yoghurt that has been strained in a cloth (muslin) to remove the whey and to give it a creamy consistency.

ZUCCHINI also called courgette; small, pale- or dark-green or yellow vegetable of the squash family.

INDEX

This book is published in 2015 by Octopus Publishing Group Limited
based on materials licensed to it by Bauer Media Books, Australia

Bauer Media Books is a division of Bauer Media Pty Limited.

54 Park St, Sydney; GPO Box 4088, Sydney, NSW 2001, Australia

phone (+61) 2 9282 8618; fax (+61) 2 9126 3702

www.awwcookbooks.com.au

MEDIA GROUP

BAUER MEDIA BOOKS

Publisher – Jo Runciman

Editorial & food director – Pamela Clark

Director of sales, marketing & rights – Brian Cearnes

Creative director & designer – Hieu Chi Nguyen

Junior editor – Amy Bayliss

Recipe editor – Rebecca Meli

Published and Distributed in the United Kingdom by Octopus Publishing Group

Carmelite House

50 Victoria Embankment

London, EC4Y 0DZ

United Kingdom

info@octopus-publishing.co.uk

www.octopusbooks.co.uk

Printed by Toppan Printing Co., China

International foreign language rights, Brian Cearnes, Bauer Media Books bcearnes@bauer-media.com.au

A catalogue record for this book is available from the British Library.
ISBN: 978 1909770 263 (paperback)